Illustrations Jozien Koelewijn
Photography DC George and Koelewijn
Design & layout www.creative kingdom.nl
Editor Jenny Franklin

Acknowledgements

There are so many people to thank, some who are still with us and some who are not.

Special thanks to Wilson and Grace Goeda, founders of YWAM Durban, who gave me this opportunity and supported me along the way. To all at YWAM Durban , especially my friends Kim and Johanna and yes, to you Ben (even though you only came along at the end).

Thanks to all my family, friends and supporters. You helped make this possible.

And of course thanks to the women of Burlington for opening up, for sharing your hearts and your stories. Above all this book is for you.

Introduction

Burlington is an informal settlement in the suburbs of Durban, South Africa, home to approximately 6000 people – the majority of them Zulu. Nestled deep in a valley, the small government houses and cheek-by-jowl makeshift shacks squat in direct contrast to the far more extravagant houses ranging up the neighbouring hill – a constant reminder of the stark inequality and discrimination that exists in South Africa.

Heaving with people night and day, Burlington is a far from peaceful and orderly place. Its chaotic heartbeat pulses throughout the surrounding environment, a never-silent groundswell of noise, a resounding drumbeat which alerts all to its existence.

In this impoverished community, the people face challenges every day – unemployment, poverty, violence, crime, sickness and the reality of HIV/Aids.

Yet amidst such desperate circumstances,
Amidst hourly reports of people being hurt,
The chaos of the weekend,
The drinking and the smoking of drugs,
It is here you will find many whose hearts are pure as gold,
Whose lives defy and overcome insurmountable odds.

Our lives are made up of stories,
Yours and mine
Some are happy
Some are sad
Some are forgotten
And some have still not found their end.

Our lives are made up of stories,
Yours and mine
Yet none of them stand alone.
Each one is part of our ongoing journey
Moulding us
Shaping us
Into the person
God intended us to become.

Our lives are made up of stories,
Yours and mine
Each connected to the other
In a never ending tapestry
Traceable through generations
Spread throughout the world.

Our lives are made up of stories,
Yours and mine
And if we take the time
To learn from one another's
It will help us in our own.
For a story will take us places
That we cannot go alone

Mama Lungi's Story

There is a story that I want to tell. It's a story about a woman who captured my heart; a story about a woman I wish was still here. She did not get the chance to tell it, and I am honoured to be telling it for her. In doing so, I know that she will live on in our hearts forever.

Her name was Mama Lungi, and it was in Burlington, where our stories find their home, that I met her. The intense heat of the Durban sun was beating down on my back as I walked through the settlement that day. That day I was walking door to door, introducing myself to the different families that lived there. I was just raising my hand to knock on the next door that I had come to, my fist clenched in mid air, when my attention was suddenly stolen elsewhere.

'Are you Grace?' someone asked.

Turning in the direction of the voice, I saw a woman rushing towards me. I opened my mouth to speak, but did not have time.

'Can you help me?' she gasped as she forced the words out between long laborious breaths.

She reached out and grabbed my arm, pulling me away from where I was standing. I felt immediately drawn towards this woman, willingly walking with her as she urged me on. The asthma inhaler that she held in her hand explained her difficulty in breathing.

'What's your name?' I asked as we walked along the dirt road together.

'Lungi,' she answered, steering us towards a small house. 'This is where I live. Please, come in.'

The house was much like the many others I had visited in Burlington. Like them, this one was small, with only two rooms. A quick glance around showed a double bed which took up most of the space, indicating that the room served as a bedroom by night, while the two plate stove along the far side of the wall implied that it was also the main living room and kitchen.

'Please, sit,' Lungi said gesturing towards a rickety old chair, occupying a small space beside the bed. I sat down, glad for a moments rest in what was becoming an increasingly hot day.

'How many people are living here?' I asked.

Lungi pulled out a photo album from a small drawer beside the bed and began showing me pictures of her family.

I listened with growing amazement as she listed all the people living with her. Mama Lungi was blessed with five children of her own. Some were already grown, yet all lived at home. She had three small grandchildren with her, and a further two children had come to stay when one of her two sisters had passed away from HIV/Aids. Another two children belonging to her brother had also come to call this home. Lastly, her only living sister, Elisabeth, was also resident. By the time she finally stopped, I had counted fourteen in total.

I looked around me in astonishment, wondering where everybody slept. As if hearing my thoughts, Mama Lungi pointed to the only other room in the small abode, leading off to our left. 'That is where the men sleep,' she said. Then she patted the bed on which she sat, indicating the room at large. 'And this is where the women and children sleep.'

While she spoke, some of the younger inhabitants of the house appeared at the door, shrinking back as they encountered an unfamiliar face in their home. From what they considered a safe distance, they peered in, only the tops of their heads and their eyes visible from where I sat. Lungi began to get up from the bed, meaning to shoo the children away, but pre-empting her intention I lifted my arm to stop her.

'No, let them come in,' I insisted, 'I would love to meet your family.'

Mama Lungi was a very special lady, and she and her family became an important part of my life. From our first encounter it was clear that many people looked to her for help and that her big heart was filled with love for all who crossed her path; she was Mother to many.

That day she asked me to help her support her family.

Mama Lungi was a keen baker: having learnt the basics in a previous job, she had developed quite a passion for it. Without fail, she would be first to bake the cake for any special occasion. To my amazement, she had devised a way to bake bread on that two plate stove in her small kitchen! Now she had put these skills to good use, baking and selling bread for 50c a slice to the children in Burlington.

However, Mama Lungi was ill. It had become a struggle to bake enough bread to provide for her ever-growing family. The burden fell heavily upon her, putting more and more strain on her physical health. She was visiting the hospital more and more. On one such occasion, they diagnosed her with Tuberculosis. Hearing this, I decided that I must address the issue of her health further.

'Lungi,' I said, looking straight into her eyes, 'I think that you should have an HIV/Aids test.'

When the result came back, it was positive.

She was admitted to hospital that day and when I went to visit her, I was faced with the harsh reality of HIV/Aids in South Africa. Entering the ward, I felt the air become heavy, and a strong sense of foreboding fell on me.

The image of David and Goliath flashed through my mind; the tale of a little boy who faces an undefeated giant. In that moment I understood HIV/Aids to be that Giant: I was in his world. I heard his sinister laugh loud in my ear, mocking me as he bellowed, 'I am HIV/Aids and you are entering my domain!' The evil way in which he spoke these words caused my whole body to tremble. But David had defeated Goliath! Armed with this knowledge, I refused to be intimidated. Taking a deep breath and lifting my head high, I walked directly into the middle of the battle field, in search of Mama Lungi.

Countless faces, all with the same tortured expression, filled the room. Most of them would die in that room, and they knew it. I noticed a sign fixed to the wall, and a wave of nausea came over me as I read its grim words. 'Do not leave your family alone' it forewarned in bold letters. Apparently the 'or you may not find them alive when you return' was not deemed a necessary addition.

Everyone was waiting, though for what they seemed unclear. Some appeared eager for death to arrive and release them from their present suffering, despite the unknown of where it would take them. Some wanted to run far, far away: since this was not a possibility, they were trying in vain to disappear within themselves and hide. Visitors were scarce and most faced the unknown alone. The certainty of death was inescapable, its existence all around, saturating the very air. The thought of Mama Lungi alone in this place was unbearable, though it was the reality for most.

Eventually I found her, one amongst many others. What I saw grieved my spirit. She was so restless. She appeared to be trying to escape her own body, to climb out and run away. In her frustration she repeatedly got up from the bed and walked back and forth around it, clearly agitated by the endless wailing of those around her. I think if she had possessed the strength she would have put on her coat and her shoes and walked out of there. She so badly wanted to communicate, but was unable to talk through the oxygen mask enabling her to breathe. As I looked into her eyes, she silently implored me to take her far away from that hopeless place.

I wish that I had.

I sat with her for a time. How desperately I wished that there was something I could do to ease her suffering but, utterly helpless, I eventually got up to leave. As I leant over the bed to kiss her goodnight, she took my hand in hers. I was surprised at the strength of her grip. With the other hand, she snatched the oxygen mask from her mouth, quickly splattering out her words before having to replace it.

'Say a prayer for me,' she asked, her voice frail under her laboured breaths. Happy to finally do something for her, I prayed God's peace would descend upon her.

She appeared to settle some as I did.

I returned to the hospital early the next morning, taking Mama Lungi's sister along with me. Pulling into the hospital car park, an uneasy feeling stirred in the pit of my stomach. I tried to ignore it. Finding my way back to the ward where I had left her the night before, I walked straight to Mama Lungi's bed.

She was not there.

I looked around the room, checking each bed as I did - there was no sign of her. The uneasy feeling in my stomach increased. Finding a nurse, I asked where they had moved her. She looked back at me blankly. As if my request in such a place was quite ridiculous. She sent us to another ward to find out if Mama Lungi had been moved. I suspect she knew our efforts would be in vain.

We looked in many wards, all of them alike. In each one we discovered more people, all of them with that same tortured expression. The more I saw, the more my hope wavered. I approached the nursing staff again. I explained the situation, yet again, and as I did so one of the nurses reached for a thick book of death certificates. Later I would learn they were all from the previous twenty four hours. She flicked through the book, her casual manner conveying her close intimacy with death. She checked each name, while I tried desperately to read them myself.

Then she paused at one page and discreetly folded back the bottom corner.

She said nothing. She didn't have to. She continued to go through the motions of turning the pages, and reaching the end of the

Wendy's Story

From the day he was born,
I knew I would watch my son die.

Strangely enough, he seemed brighter the day it finally happened. I even allowed the thought to cross my mind that perhaps he was getting a little better. 'Mama, can I have some eggs?' he asked softly. I was so pleased to hear he had an appetite! After helping him eat, I pulled the cover straight and fluffed his pillow to make him comfortable. His small frame sunk down on the bed. He looked up at me. 'Mama,' he asked, 'will you carry me on your back?' Just like I had done when he was a baby.

I did not realise then what he was really asking. Young as he was, my son knew he did not have much time left. He wanted to feel close to me one more time. To know the comfort and security of his mother one last time. To be taken back to a time when sickness and death still seemed so far away. But I did not catch the meaning of his request. 'What!' I replied jokingly. 'Such a tall man like you? No way!'

I did not know I was going to regret that decision for the rest of my life.

It happened so fast. The sense of comfort I had felt earlier that day, when he appeared brighter, quickly faded. But then the hiccups started. 'This child is surely dying!' my neighbour insisted. 'Take him to the hospital straight away.'

I did not want to hear her words. Yet how could I ignore them? Looking at my son lying on his bed, I could see how small he was.

Six years old, but so thin. I knew he was weak. I knew he had been weak for quite some time, but really the only difference I could see now were the hiccups. I did not want to take him back to the hospital. He had spent so much of his short life there! But I could not take any chances.

His father was working far away and so a friend agreed to drive us. I held him in my arms all the way, holding him close, praying. His hiccups were getting worse. I could see that my neighbour was right. Something was different with him now. I sensed that he was slipping away.

I jumped out of the car before it stopped and charged through the hospital door, straight into a doctor. He grabbed hold of my shoulders, gently pushed me back a few steps, and looked into my face. From there he looked down at my son, whom I still held tight in my arms.

'What is it, Mama?' he asked. 'What is it?'

I tried to speak, but could not form the words in my mouth. I felt my son's breath, so hot on my chest. Suddenly I feared it might be his last.

All of a sudden people were around me, taking my son from my arms. As they did, I could feel all the strength being sucked out of my body and I almost fell to the floor. But love for my son beat through me and, pulling myself straight, I chased after them.

My eyes were fixed on the small part of him that I could still see as they rushed him into a room up ahead. Following closely behind, I watched as they fixed tubes and an oxygen mask to his small body. To help him? It all seemed to be a pretence - as if they were trying to trick me, as if they did not want to let me know what was really going on.

Pushing at them to get past, I cried, 'No, move! I'll do it myself!'

I felt someone take hold of my shoulders, pulling me backwards, away from him. I did not have the strength to fight, and bowed my head as I was led out of the room. Stumbling out of the door, I looked back over my shoulder and saw that my son's eyes were wide open. I hoped that this was a good sign.

Then they closed the door behind me. I saw him no more.

I felt people's eyes on me as I stood there in the hospital corridor, and it is true that I was a strange sight. I had put on such a short dress that day, and gradually it had crept further and further up, until it was now sitting around my waist, revealing my underwear for all to see. Quickly I pulled the dress down and folded my arms across my chest.

I could not take my eyes away from the closed door. I was lost in my pain, knowing that my son was inside and there was nothing I could do to help him. It took me a few moments to hear the sobs filling the air around me. Finally I tore my eyes away from the door and looked at the women crying near me and I wondered what tragedy caused their tears. I did not realise that it was my tragedy, and that I was the only one who did not understand.

I stood there, refusing to see what they already knew. My son was already gone. Then an uncle approached me.

'Come my daughter,' he said, putting his arm around my shoulders. Gently he led me to a chair and sitting on it, he pulled me down with him. Like a little girl, I sat there on his knee. 'Everything is going to be ok, my child,' he said over and over again, 'everything is going to be ok.'

The words washed over me - surprisingly soothing. And I was beginning to believe there was some truth to them, when my child's father arrived.

He burst into the ward and his sudden presence shocked me back to reality. Jumping up from the uncle's knee, I walked quickly towards him. Single-minded, he gave me his attention only long enough to find out where his son was, and then he saw me no more. He banged on the door, he tried to get into the room, but it was clear that no matter how long or how hard he banged, they were not going to let him in.

Angry, distressed, he could not restrain the emotion raging inside of him and security had to be called to escort him out of the ward. Following him outside, I tried to calm him down, but my words were pointless. I had trouble believing them myself. 'It will be ok,' I said. Still, the words would not have comforted either of us for long. A small body bag was wheeled out, and passed right in front of us.

No one had to tell me that it was my son.

I was sixteen years old when I discovered I was pregnant. Only a child myself, some might say, though I had been forced to grow up fast. My childhood was not what you might call easy, or secure. In fact, all I remember is arguing and fighting in our household. The problem was that both my mother and my father were alcoholics and neither was faithful to the other. In the end, any love that they had for one another grew cold and was replaced with hate. I was only seven years old when they separated for good.

After they split, life only got worse for me and my siblings. Neither parent took responsibility for us. Unfortunately, both of them were more interested in finding another partner than in us, and our lives became more and more and more unstable.

At first, we lived with our father. But one day he decided that he wanted to marry his latest girl-friend. This was not good news for us. His new wife, not happy about acquiring five more children to add to her own, chased us all away.

One by one we all went in search of our mother, although we did not know where to start. She never stayed in one place for long, and when we eventually found her, we never knew whether she would be gone when we got home from school. And that is exactly what happened. Arriving home one day, I discovered that she had been fired from her job and told to leave her live-in quarters. I had no way of knowing where she had gone to. I stayed with a friend that night and thankfully my younger brother turned up at my school the next day. This time he had been sent to tell me where they had moved to.

Unfortunately she did not always tell us. On the final occasion, she left my brother and me to fend for ourselves. My other siblings had gone off as well; we seemed to have trouble staying together as a family. I was about fifteen at the time and my brother was no older than seven. There was rent to pay, food to buy. We lived in fear, as every night a man came banging on our door, having drunk too much beer. It was left to me to figure out a solution.

Following my mother's example, I found myself a boyfriend.

He was older than I was, but that did not matter at the time. I was simply happy that we had someone to look after us. Although my brother did not stay with us long. I was persuaded that things would be better for him if I contacted welfare and had him placed with a family; one that would be able to provide for all his needs. I thought it was best for him. It was hard to let him go, but I met with the couple who were to look after him and I was certain life with them would be better than anything I could provide for him.

Now there was only myself to worry about.

My boyfriend took me home to his parent's house. I remember thinking that they had a nice house, certainly more comfortable than any home I had ever had. My boyfriend's mother was very kind to me and treated me as though I was her last born. It was the first time that I had experienced love in my life and for a short time there ensued a period of stability. But the stability did not last long and soon my world crumbled again. My boyfriend - he was a ladies man you see.

It was during this time that I found out I was pregnant with my son.

I wish that was all that I discovered.
I also discovered I was HIV-positive.

The weight of the news fell heavy upon my shoulders; a weight that has been there ever since; a death sentence hanging over my life. At only sixteen, my life was over before it had even started.

As for me and my 'ladies man' of a boyfriend, we did not stay together long after my son was born. He had once been engaged, but he had broken it off because his fiancé had been unfaithful to him. A joke, considering his own infidelities. However, I found out they were back together, even though he was supposed to be with me! I knew he was serious about marrying her, for he had paid *lobola* (bride price) and so, realising I was wasting my time, I left.

Of course it was bad enough that I had the virus, but worse was the news that my son had contracted it also. He was such a beautiful baby boy. He looked so healthy at first, but it was not long until I saw the effects of the virus on his body. No matter what we did and how many doctors we took him to see, he was never going to live very long.

My son stayed at his father's house, where I knew they would be able to take better care of him. Of course I visited him often and as his condition worsened I moved back to be with him. However when my son died, I returned to my mother, who by this time was living here in Burlington. That is how I came to be here you see.

Of course, my mother had not changed and it was not long until she disappeared again.

I was not surprised when she left, but at least this time I was old enough to look after myself. Though I was never alone for long in my life and soon I met someone else. His name was Joseph. I was scared to tell him about my HIV status at first, but I found out that his wife had died from Aids and therefore I was not the one to give it to him. He refused to talk about it, although I am sure deep down he knew that he had it. I did try to talk to him about it, time and time again. Once when I had TB, I tried, but he knew what I was going to say and would not let me speak. I think he thought that if we did not talk about it, then somehow it would not be real.

I wish that were the case.

In my life, HIV has taken the people that I love most. I watched my son die. Not long afterwards I also watched Jo die. When I met him, he was a big, tough man, but he became a shadow of himself. I had to do everything for him. In the end he could not move or even talk. When the ambulance came to take him to the hospital, there was little hope that he would ever return.

Jo had two daughters and that night we all huddled together, each one of us silently offering a prayer heavenwards as we waited for news. It was early in the morning and still dark when the phone rang. I was only sleeping lightly and as soon as I heard it, I quickly got out of the bed to answer it, taking care not to wake the children who had finally fallen asleep. I knew that a phone call at such an early hour would not be good news. I knew that the end had been inevitable, but it had not seemed to register that he was actually dying. Like it had been with my son, I did not want to see the reality. Hearing the nurse actually speak the words out loud, I crumpled to the ground.

I remained outside for a time. I tried to gather my thoughts and fight the emotions welling up inside of me. I knew I had to stay strong for the girls and I was determined to do this one last thing for Jo. Yet how do you gently tell two young girls that their father is dead, when their mother is dead already?

I found them sitting up in bed waiting for me, staring at me with big wide eyes. Taking a deep breath, I let the words fall out of my mouth. Their cries invaded the stillness of that early morning, alerting all who heard them that death had visited our home once more.

Now it is my turn to be sick.
I am twenty five years old.
And I do not know how much longer I will live.

So what would you think if a sixteen year old girl told you
she was HIV positive?
Would you look down on her?
Would you pity her?
Would you think she was dirty?
Tell me, what would you think?
What would you see?

I'll tell you what people think. I'll tell you what I see in their eyes when they look at me.

They think that I am dirty. They think that I'm unclean, that I should have been more careful and I only have myself to blame.

But I am here to tell them, I never wanted this life. No, I never wanted it to turn out this way.

I am here to tell them that behind this virus there is person, a life and a story. And maybe it is time that they opened their eyes to see me, to see the circumstances of life that have led me here to this place, this place where I find myself today.

I am here today because I never knew love as a child. My mother never loved me; my father never loved me. Neither of them looked after me as they ought.

I am here today because I wanted to survive. I doubt you even have ears to believe all I have done, just to make it through the days, the months and the years.

I am here today because really there seemed to be no other way. My life has played out before me, neither asking nor giving me a choice.

You see, life has been hard. By the time this body was fifteen years of age, it had been raped five times. I did not understand why; I only knew that it was wrong. I did not tell anyone, because there was no one safe to tell.

Yes, life has been hard. I have lost people along the way; first my mother, then my son and then the love of my life Jo. But I have had to keep going, I have had to be strong for my brothers and my sisters, for the people left behind with me. And I am determined to keep on going and never give up. The world is very big and I am simply not finished yet: there is so much more that I want to do, there is so much more that I want to see.

I know that the opposition is fierce. I know that the devil does not want me to make it. He wants to take me out. But I am holding on tight and I have no intention of letting go, not yet anyway. I know that Jesus is the One, and He is on my side, in this pit, fighting alongside me.

So my friends, if you meet someone with Aids or HIV, remember me.

Remember a girl by the name of Wendy Slindile Kuzwayo and all that I have told you.

Remember that there is more to me, far more than what you may first perceive.

Remember that behind this virus, there is a person, a life and a story, waiting for you to see.

Remember that there is more to me than Aids and HIV.

Nomvula's Story

We call them the tokoloshe – the evil spirits feared by many Zulu people. If you go into many of the homes here in Burlington, you will see our beds raised up off the ground on bricks, so that the small dwarf-like tokoloshe can't get to us while we sleep.

Now I can't say for sure whether it was the tokoloshe that tormented me. I don't think it matters what name we give them. All I know is that whatever they were – they were very real and very evil.

It is said that the tokoloshe are only visible to children, and I was seven years old when it first revealed itself to me. I was at school that day. The teacher was busy writing on the board, with his back to the class. I was sitting at my desk, when suddenly, my school bag started moving.

Can you imagine my surprise? It literally started moving, edging away from me little by little, all by itself! At first all I did was stare at it, not knowing what to think or do. Then I stole some glances around me to see if anyone else had noticed. No one had. Each one of them was carrying on as normal, eyes fixed forward, attention on the teacher.

I felt compelled to get up and follow my bag as it inched further away from me. I walked out of the classroom and out of the school entirely. No one noticed or stopped me. I simply followed the small, dwarf-like man who was now carrying my bag.

Next thing I knew I was waking up under a bush, far from school and from my home.

It was dark when I woke. My mind flooded with confusion, which slowly turned to fear. I could not remember having fallen asleep. I peered through the darkness trying to figure out where I was. Searching my memory, I tried to piece together what had happened, but nothing came to mind. Disorientated and unsettled I found my way back to the main road, and grabbed the arm of the first passer-by that I met. It was a woman, and she peered at me through the darkness, probably wondering what a young girl was doing out so late on her own. I asked her the time and she told me that it was already passed seven in the evening. I was shocked! At once, I turned on my heel and ran for home, knowing that trouble awaited me there.

Sure enough, my mother was waiting for me at the door of our home, having seen me approach from a distance.

'Where have you been? You should have been home from school hours ago!' she shouted.

Of course, I tried to explain what had happened, although I was not entirely sure myself. The words tripped over themselves as they nervously fell out of my mouth, and the expression on my mother's face grew more and more agitated as I spoke. I could see that she thought I was making up elaborate stories in an attempt to get myself out of trouble. She scolded me, and demanded that I tell her where I had really been. But what could I say? The truth seemed unbelievable even to me. I gave up trying and just accepted my mother's fury.

She thrust a plate of now cold food in front of me and I forced myself to eat whilst inside I was battling the rising fear and confusion. If I had known that this was merely the beginning of my problems, I would not have been able to eat at all.

From that day on, the evil spirits visited me on a regular basis.

Day after day they came, each time isolating me more and more, drawing me further away from my family and friends. As time went by, I stopped playing with other children, no longer joining in with their games. Soon it became a rarity for me to be in school and when I was, I could barely concentrate. As for my family, they passed me off as a naughty and uncontrollable child and did not believe my stories, so eventually I stopped trying to communicate with anyone at all. It felt as though only the tokoloshe understood me, so it was easier to spend time with them. At least when they got their own way that is, and did not become violent – which they often did.

The tokoloshe were powerful you see, and much stronger than me. I did not have the strength to stand up to them and I would often experience their wrath. Many times they asked me to get food for them. Having learnt that it was not good to disobey them, I followed their orders. My mother would fill my plate with food and I would go outside and give it to the tokoloshe. However, over time she became suspicious. Returning to her one day, my plate empty, I asked for more.

'Who are you giving this food to?' she exclaimed, hands on her hips as she looked from me to the empty plate in my hand and back again.

The steely look in her eyes demanded an answer. However, I could only stare back at her, at a loss for words. I had tried before to tell her about the evil spirits, but these attempts had not been met favourably, and this time I thought it best to keep my mouth shut.

'Well, no more food,' she said, and I could tell by the look on her face that there would be no convincing her. With the empty plate in my hand, I walked back outside, fear churning inside me, for I knew the tokoloshe was not going to be happy.

Sure enough, he was standing where I had left him, waiting for his food. When he saw the empty plate, he raised his hand high above his head. Clenching it into a fist, he brought it down with full force, right into the side of my face. The blow threw me off my feet and onto the dusty ground. Before I had the chance to catch my breath, he came straight at me and grabbing me by the shirt he pulled me to my feet. My legs buckled beneath me as he brought his fist down, again and again onto the side of my face. I dropped to my knees. He kept hitting me, over and over again, and my mouth was full of blood by the time he stopped. Eventually he let me go and I fell backwards onto the ground - a battered mess. Then he was gone.

I lay there for a long time. Every so often I tried to open my eyes, but my vision blurred and the glare of the sun sent a searing pain through my head. I stayed there, utterly alone.

The day was beginning to cool off as the sun retreated for the day by the time I finally managed to pull myself up off the ground and move back towards the house. I was able to see more clearly now, although my body was throbbing with pain. I lifted my hand to my face and winced at my own touch. Walking into my family's house, I saw my mother busy cooking supper at the stove. Hearing me approach, she lifted her head in my direction. The familiar glint in her eye told me that she was not happy.

'Girl, where...' she began, but the words dried up as her eyes surveyed my swollen and bruised face.

From that day on, my mother believed me. At first, my mother tried to help me.

In my culture, traditionally we consult a *sangoma* (witch doctor) and *inyanga* (herbalist) for help in such matters. So my mother decided that I should see an *inyanga*; and with no choice in the matter, I went. The *inyanga* made small cuts all over my body. I don't know why he did this, but he said it would help fight the evil spirits. He also mixed together a *muthi* (medicine) which he gave to my mother. He told her she must take it home, boil it and then give it to me to drink. He said it would cause me to vomit the spirits out of my body. The *inyanga* assured both me and my mother that this would make everything right and after paying him for his time, we took the prescribed *muthi* and went home. Eagerly I followed the *inyanga's* instructions.

Unfortunately, it didn't work.

Then one day my grandmother called me to her. Obediently I walked over to where she sat. Reaching towards me, she took hold of my arms and pulled me close. She looked me straight in the eye.

'The *sangoma* and *inyanga*, they cannot help you, child. Only God can. If He wants to help you He will, if not then so be it,' she said. She pulled out a rosary from her pocket and put it in my hand. Closing my hand around it with her own, she assured me, 'This will protect you from the spirits, child.' With that it was clear she had no more to say to me, so I took myself away outside.

Once outside, I leaned against the wall of our house and slowly slid down it until I was sitting on the ground, my knees hunched up against me. I opened my hand and looked at the rosary my grandmother had placed there. A sense of hope tentatively stirred inside of me as I wondered if this was the answer; whether this would actually ward off the evil spirits.

But just like the *inyanga's muthi*, the rosary proved incapable of protecting me.

My life spun slowly more and more out of control, and by the time I was ten years old I spent more time away from home than there. I lived on the streets a lot of the time, and it was during such a time that I found a place of refuge for a while. It was a home for street kids like me, run by three pastors. One was from America, one was Indian and the other African. In this place I was treated with more care than I had ever experienced before, and it was also in this place that I began to learn of a power far greater than that of the evil spirits.

I had not been at the home long when once again I heard the evil spirits calling my name. It was late at night and though I was already in bed, I knew that I had to obey. So throwing the covers off, I walked to the front door of the home. I was about to open the door and walk outside to the spirits, when one of the pastors stopped me. He put his hand on my raised arm and asked me where I was going at such an hour. He was not angry, as I expected; instead he seemed concerned. I told him that the evil spirits were calling my name and that I must obey, otherwise they would hurt me. On hearing this, the pastor crouched down so that he was able to look directly into my eyes.

'You do not need to listen to the spirits anymore, you are safe here,' he said in a reassuring voice.

Initially I was not convinced by his words, but as he prayed for me there at the front door, something inside told me that maybe I could believe this man. He then led me back to my room and I crawled into bed. That night I slept more soundly than I had in a long time.

From that day on and during my entire stay at the home, I was safe; the spirits did not visit me. I never ventured out, as I did not want to risk the spirits returning. Then one day, after I had been there for almost a year and a half, a friend persuaded me to go with her to town. I hesitated; it had been so long since I had been anywhere. But my friend was persistent.

'Come on,' she said, 'it'll be fun!'

I was unsure, but my long absence from the outside world eventually enticed me out of hiding, and I made the decision to go. I convinced myself that the evil spirits were gone now, and that I had nothing to worry about.

I really enjoyed being back in amongst people and the busyness of town. It had been so long. However, I had forgotten to be on guard and I was taken by surprise when I felt a hand grip my shoulder. Turning around I looked up into the face of my aunt. Regret instantly washed over me as I knew that she was not going to let me go.

'Child', she exclaimed, 'where have you been?'

I did not answer and merely hung my head, staring at my feet. She must have realised that any further questions would prove futile, as she did not ask any more.

'You are coming home with me!' she said simply as she began to pull me by the arm through the busy street.

I did not want to go home, and as my aunt pulled me along a sense of dread welled up inside of me. I had no desire to see my family, especially not my mother, and I sensed the feeling was mutual. As we got closer to my house I wondered what my mother's reaction would be.

For a moment I thought that maybe things would be different, now that the evil spirits had left my life. However as soon as I saw my mother's face, I knew that such thoughts were foolish. For in the moment before she managed to conceal it with a smile, her face gave away the disappointment she felt at seeing me. Her body seemed to literally sink, as though the weight of my return physically fell on her. I could see in her eyes that my homecoming caused her more distress than joy.

I had not been home long when I also learned that I was wrong about the spirits being gone from my life. For almost as soon as I returned, so did they. They had been waiting for an opportune time to sneak back into my life. While I was at the home I had been safe, as the pastors had a power that outmatched that of the spirits. Yet at home I was alone, and despite my family's physical proximity, there was no one to protect me. And I did not know how to protect myself.

Life carried on like this for a long time. Each day rolled into the next, and each new morning turned into another day to survive. Then on one not so different day, my mother told me that it was time for me to be married.

'You must have your own house and life away from here,' she said.

The next thing I knew *lobola* (bride price) had been paid - eleven cows in total. This is how it is done in Zulu culture. There was no big wedding or celebration, but all at once I was leaving my family and joining a new one, as somebody's wife. I was only fifteen years old, and not only was I now a new wife, I was soon to become a young mother as well. I suppose I should have been scared or angry, but truly I did not feel much of anything. Life these days was something that happened to me. Rather than being an active participant, I watched from the sidelines with nothing to offer.

By the time I was married, the tokoloshe no longer appeared to me. I was too old you see. But I knew the evil spirits were still there. They weighed heavy on me, pulling me down. I knew that they were on my back, driving me to live a life of destruction. Somewhere along the way I started drinking. I can't give you a specific reason why, it was more that it just happened than by any definite choice to do so. I had no respect for myself, or for other people. I did not feel loved or have any love inside of me to give. I lived my life simply going through the motions.

Then one day a man of God from Pretoria came to Durban. He set up a big tent and he held meetings there every night for a month. I was curious more than anything else, and so I went along one evening. I had not been in there long when the pastor looked in my direction. It was as though he was looking through me rather than at me.

'You are not a woman, where is the owner of this body?' he cried out, and I realised that his eyes were open to more than the physical world; that he could see the evil spirits which were ruling me.

Coming towards me he began to speak directly to the spirits, telling them to leave my body. After that, I do not remember much. All I know is that when I came back to my senses, I felt a lightness that I had never had before. The pastor was standing in front of me, and this time he looked into my eyes. I felt different and I knew that this man had something to do with it. This man had the same power that I had encountered while living at the home. While I do not remember much, I am told that while I was unconscious my body was overwhelmed by spirits, and I fought everyone in sight. But the people were not put off by what they saw manifest in me. They knew that they had a power far greater than what they were dealing with and were convinced enough to use it.

I went back every night after that, drawn to the power that I saw in these people and the God they talked about. However, they were only there for a month and then they left. I did not know how to stay strong on my own and with no one to encourage me, I stopped praying and I stopped reading the Bible. That's when the spirits saw their chance. They came back with force and drove my life once again. I started drinking again, worse than before.

However, I did begin to make some changes in my life. One day, as though a veil lifted from my eyes, I suddenly saw how much older my husband was than me. I realised that I only existed to give him children. Pregnant with my third child, I took my two children and left. Of course, my husband was not happy, although I don't think that it was because he loved either me or our children. He was angry because he had paid *lobola* and that was seen as a binding contract, tying me to him. Now if I was going to leave him, he wanted his money back.

He took me to court but his efforts were futile as I had been underage when I married him and the magistrate let me go. My husband was ordered to pay child maintenance, but he never did. Nor did I try to make him. I wanted to get on with my life and I did not want anything from him. So I found myself a job and rented a home for me and my children.

I did not stay single long. It was during a time in my life that I was searching, when something inside pushed me to look for more than what I had always known. Even though I was always looking in the wrong places. This new man was just like everyone else and he tried to control me.

'Do this, get me that, don't wear that, wear this,' he said. I put up with it for a time; I was used to it you see and I suppose I loved him, as much as I could love anyone then.

However one day I thought, 'Enough!' Going to my boyfriend's home, I told him that I did not want to see him anymore.

'I don't love you,' I said, looking him straight in the eye.

I could almost see the anger welling up inside of him at the sound of my words, taking over every inch of his body until his eyes darkened with threatening intent. He pounced on me, his rage dictating his actions. Rage that infused his body with such strength that I was left defenceless against his torrent of punches. For three weeks he kept me there. He would leave for work in the morning and lock me inside, imprisoned like an animal. I had no choice but to stay there, writhing in agony, waiting fearfully for his return, wondering if this time he would actually kill me.

One day I was in so much pain, all I could manage to do was offer a silent prayer up to heaven.

'Please God,' I asked, ' if it is my time to die then let it be now – right now, as I cannot take the pain much longer. But if you want to help me, then please make it soon.'

I know God heard my prayer, for the next day when my boyfriend left for work, he forgot to lock the door behind him. I waited a little while, till I knew that he was definitely gone and not waiting outside. Then I made my escape.

I managed to get to the main road, willing myself to keep going as every step I took sent excruciating pains throughout my body. Thank God that the first car to pass by stopped, as many would have kept on driving after seeing the mess that I was in. They took me to the nearby police station and from there directly to the hospital. I spent three months in the hospital recovering. I don't know what would have happened if I had not escaped when I did. I very much doubt I would be here to tell you the tale. Even now I still have problems with my body because of it. I can show you my wrists and I can show you my ankles and there you will see the scars. That is where he tied the ropes so tightly that they cut deep into my skin.

The doctors tried to persuade me to stay longer in the hospital, but I discharged myself. I had spent long enough there, and I wanted to get back to my children. However, I did not want to go back to Umlazi, the township where we were living at the time. The police had not caught up with my boyfriend and I needed to make sure that my children would be safe. So I came here to Burlington. And it was here that I met another man.

I thought Wilfrid was different. I thought he was a good man. I believed he would take care of me and my children. He said all the right things. He said he believed in God and although I was not ready to surrender my all to Him, I thought Wilfrid might help me get to a place where I was. I was wrong. It was all just words. He lied to me; he did not treat me with the respect I now know I deserve. It is not easy to hide anything in Burlington, and someone told me that Wilfred was seeing another woman.

I did not know what to do when I first heard these words. I did not want to believe them, but something inside told me it was true.

Still I had to see for myself, to make sure. I was told where they were and I went straight to the house. I knocked on the door, but nobody answered.

I knocked again. Still there was no response. The anger began to boil inside of me, and I was determined to get in. I started kicking the door with my foot. The door was weak, so it did not take much to force my way in.

And there they were - eyes wide as they watched me barge into the house. I watched as Wilfred stood up and came toward me. He began to speak, but his words did not register with me. All I could hear was my own rage ringing in my ears, drowning everything else out. I went straight for him and aimed the stick I was holding at his head, but somehow he managed to duck from under me and out the door. He left that day and never came back

As for the woman, well she ran too, leaving Burlington for a short while. Perhaps she thought I would calm down with time. But my anger did not go away, in fact the time only served to intensify it. On the day I heard she had returned to Burlington, I made my way to her house. Walking through the door, I started to tear the place apart. Whatever my hands found, I smashed against the wall or threw to the ground.

I pulled everything out of the cupboards, cups and plates crashed to the floor. Picking up the television, I threw it out the door into the street, not caring if someone was walking passed. I did not stop until everything had been destroyed.

The woman was cowering in the corner, unable to get past me to escape. Picking up a broken bottle from the floor, I turned my attention towards her. The house was silent now, with only the sound of the debris crunching beneath my feet as I stepped toward her.

She looked up and I saw the fear in her eyes, but it did not stop me. I smashed the bottle down over and over onto her head, stopping only when my anger finally subsided. Then, letting the bottle drop from my hand, I turned around and walked out of the house. I did not know how badly she was injured, and I did not care. I just left her there.

As I walked towards my house, I heard sirens and I figured that someone must have called the police. Later they came to arrest me. They took me to the station and I told them the whole story. They did not keep me long though, saying it was a waste of their time. They released me and I went home to my children.

It was while I was with Wilfred, that I became pregnant with my youngest child. I love all my children, but I have to say that it was different with my youngest. With my husband I knew that my only function was to bring forth his children. When I began to take charge of my own life, I began to desire things for myself, and I really wanted this baby. So I made sure that I did all the right things to look after her, and even before she was born I went for regular check-ups. It was on one of my first visits to the clinic that they tested me for HIV and I found out that I was positive.

Of course I was concerned about my unborn child, but for me? Well, I was not particularly troubled by the news. Nor did I react as expected. After spending a few moments with the counsellor, she sat back and stared at me.

'Why are you smiling?' she asked. 'Don't you understand what this means?'

'Should I scream and shout?' I replied. 'Will that make the virus disappear?'

She did not say anything after that, but simply did the minimum required of her. She gave me the information I needed to protect my baby from the virus, and then ushered me quickly out of her office. As I said, while I did not care much for my own health, I did everything that I could to protect my baby. I took the necessary tablets just before the birth and I did not breast feed her. Yet I had to wait six months before I could take her to the hospital to be tested.

She was negative. Thank God, my child was healthy.

However I still did not care about myself and I continued to live a life of destruction. From Monday through Sunday I would drink, and then I would start all over again. A bottle was never far from my hand, even as I worked. The only reason I managed to keep my job was because I was good at it.

Yet God never gave up in his pursuit of me. I can see that now. The pastor of the church here in Burlington would visit me often. He didn't care if I was drunk, which I was most of the time. On his visits he would tell me about God and though I had experienced His power before and knew it was real, I was not ready to give Him my all. The pastor encouraged me to go to church, but I did not want to go while I continued in the lifestyle that I was living. It was one way or the other, and I was not ready to try it God's way. Not yet. And I was certainly not going to go to church just to please other people.

Nobody made me change; it was simply the truth of God's Word working in my life that made me the person that I am today.

It happened one Christmas. I had plans to spend the whole of December drinking: it was all organised and the alcohol bought.

However, when the time came I felt ill and I decided not to drink. Feeling ill had never stopped me before, but somehow this time was different.

'Nomvula, why are you not drinking?' My friends asked. I did not have an answer for them. But as the days passed, without the alcohol in my system, I was able to think clearly for once. I started speaking to God and asking him questions. Why had my life been the way it had? Why had it been so hard? I did not get any clear answer, and often I still ask the same questions.

Yet something happened in that time. Maybe I had reached the end of myself, but I knew that things had to change. I thought of my children. Who would look after them if I drank myself to an early grave? So I decided to go to church and make Jesus Lord of my life. I did it for myself and for my children.

There has been no going back since then. I put my trust in God for all my needs, and yet life was still hard. People did not understand. They mocked me and said I was stupid, telling me that I was wasting my time. However, God is with me and He has made me strong. He gave me the power to persevere. I became involved in the church and learned to put God first in everything. It has been hard, but the people in the church have supported me and prayed with me.

But I knew I was still sick in my body with HIV. So I went to the clinic and they tested me again.

'No HIV,' they said.

I told them they were wrong, that they must test me again, but they said there was no mistake. I did not believe them, of course. I knew I had tested positive. So on leaving one clinic, I immediately went to another. Again they tested my blood and I waited in anticipation for the result. The same thing happened.

'Negative,' they said.

I was shocked, stunned and excited all at once. Then I thought about the power of my God and wondered why I was so surprised. God can do anything and while I do not know exactly when, He healed me. When I finally gave him permission to take over my life, he did just that. He flooded my life so completely that everything wrong in my body was put right.

When I came to Burlington I was a drunken woman, a fighter. If you did something to me that I did not like, it was easy for me to lash out and beat you. I was angry. I made so many enemies: I was forever against everyone and I did not make friends. Now I choose to love my enemies - and many cannot understand the change in me. Of course it is not always easy, but I do it because I love God. I was proud. But since I have received God, I have learned to humble myself. He has never judged me despite all my failings.

So you can see, things are different for me now. God has placed dreams in my heart: I want to go to Bible College and be a pastor. I did not go to school like other children and do not have any qualifications, yet I know that God will make a way for me. I dream one day of preaching the truth all over the world, the truth that the devil plans only to destroy and keep us from the One who loves us. I want to tell people that there is no need to be scared, that with Jesus we can do anything.

Yes, I want to preach the word of God and fight the devil until the day I die. Jesus overcomes all - I know because I have lived it! God has turned my fighting spirit into a spirit for good.

Now instead of people, I fight the devil.

was all it was to me, a Sunday outing that had to be endured - nothing more. My grandmother and my mother both had a real relationship with God, but as for me and my heart, we were not on board. You see, I only went to church because it was expected of me. God was not real to me. However, one night He decided to step into my world.

It was a seemingly normal night and I went to bed as usual, but on falling asleep I had an unusual dream. It was such a vivid dream, and I can still see it clearly to this day. I saw all this grass; such green green grass, but it was all ablaze with fire!

'How can the grass catch fire when it is so green?' I thought.

Then I heard a voice. It seemed to come from every direction all at once, surrounding me and piercing me to the core.

'That green grass is you,' the voice said. 'You are young and you like to play games! You don't know why you are going to church. But if you do not really believe in God and if you do not pray, you are going to be burnt - like that grass.'

I woke up with a start, the image of the burning grass foremost in my mind and the voice reverberating in my ears. I knew that this was not just another dream.

I jumped out of my bed and went to my grandmother. It was still early and the sun had not yet arisen, but I knew I had to speak to her straight away. I shook her, gently at first, but she did not wake. Impatiently, I shook her again, this time a little harder and she began to stir. Opening her eyes, she saw me crouching beside her, my hand still anxiously shaking her shoulder.

'What is it, child?' she asked as she began to pull herself up into a sitting position. I could see the concern creep into her eyes as she felt me trembling beside her. She put her hand on my arm and it soothed me a little. I climbed into bed beside her, and pulled her back down into the bed. With our faces so close together our noses almost touched, I began to tell her about my dream. She listened intently. Then she told me that it was time for me to make a decision.

'Are you going to carry on as you have been - playing at knowing God, or are you going to make a real commitment to Him, once and for all?'

There and then, with my grandmother by my side, I decided that I was going to give my all to Him. I have never looked back since.

Of course it has not always been easy. Many things have tried to pull me away from Him. People have told me that I am crazy. They have laughed at what they think is stupidity to put my trust in a one unseen. But my God has proved them all wrong over and over again. And it is one of these times that I want to tell you about right now.

When I got married, I did not fall pregnant for a long time. Two years passed, and still there was no baby in my womb. And with each month that I did not find myself with child, the more precarious and uncertain my situation became. It was very stressful. For you see, in my culture if a wife does not bear her husband a child, she will be returned to her parent's house and the *lobola* (bride price) repaid. My father-in-law was threatening such action and I was distraught.

My husband's family encouraged me to see a *sangoma* (witch doctor), and while I knew in my heart that it was wrong, I felt that I had no other choice. I had to look as though I was doing everything that I could and show that I indeed wanted to have a child. So I followed the *sangoma's* instructions and took the *muthi* (medicine) she prescribed. It made no difference. Another year passed, and still there was no baby.

Then one day when I was at home visiting my mother, I went to see the lady at the church I had attended as a child. She immediately knew something was wrong. I told her everything, the tears falling from my eyes. I had been holding it in for so long and it felt as though the tears would never stop. When I finally stopped sobbing, she asked me a question.

'Elsie, who do you believe more…God ... or the *sangoma* and her *muthi*?'

The question hit me hard. I realised that I had been allowing other people and my circumstances to pull me away from the truth. I fell on my knees and asked God for his forgiveness. I vowed to throw away the *sangoma's muthi* as soon as I got home and trust that, no matter what happened, God held me in the palm of his hand.

Yet this was not the only thing that she had to say.

'You know, I had a dream about you, Elsie.'

I lifted my head on hearing this. I was eager to hear what she had to say, for I knew how significant dreams could be. As she began to speak, something stirred inside me, renewing my hope as I turned my eyes back towards my God.

'In my dream I saw you with a baby girl. I believe God wants to open your womb. You and your husband must fast and pray.'

I wanted so badly to believe her, but it seemed impossible. However, I decided to follow her advice. My husband thought that I was crazy, but he agreed to go along with it.

'Let's see what this God of yours can do!' he jeered.

Although he appeared dismissive and was only going along with it to keep me happy, I knew that inwardly he was hoping this would be the answer to all our troubles.

So we fasted and we prayed. All night I cried out to the Lord, imploring him and laying bare my request. I was filled with anguish, because something inside me whispered that this was my last chance.

My husband left the next day, back to Durban for work. Yet he had not been gone one day when I started to get sick. I went to the doctor, never thinking that it could be because I was pregnant. While I trusted, I did not think that my prayers would be answered so quickly!

I wish there were words to explain my joy. I had wanted a baby so badly; it had consumed my every waking thought and even my dreams. Yet I had finally resigned myself to it not happening. I was ready to pack my bags and return to my mother's house. But God stepped in at the last minute, and my joy was all the greater for it.

After that I had lots of babies, but I have never forgotten who gave them to me and who they belong to. I have brought up my children to know Him. My children have seen that life has not been easy, especially after their father died. I don't know why God took my husband so early. I do not always understand His ways. The one thing that I do know is that God has been the husband and the father that we have needed.

I have never remarried nor have I ever taken a boyfriend. My children see this. They see how we live like people who have a father and a husband, but it is God that provides for us not a man. I have a house, but no husband. I have food, but no husband. I am eating, I am dressed and my children are looked after, but I have no husband. If I tell God what I need, for sure he never fails. If I am sick, I say 'God, your hands are not short to touch my sickness.' He listens to me when I cry and I know that He will always help me.

It was after my husband died that I moved from the Eastern Cape to Durban. I had to, in order to find work to support my many children. We moved to another township here in Durban called Ntzuma. However I was not there long, when the fighting between the ANC (African National Congress) and IFP (Inkatha Freedom Party) started.[1] I almost lost my own life and my children to the fighting, and I saw some sights that I sorely wish I could forget.

I had found a job working as a cleaner and I was on my way home from work one day, when I was met with an unusual amount of people coming in the opposite direction. At first I did not think much of it, but as I got closer to Ntzuma, people started warning me to turn back. However, my life was not worth living without my children, and knowing that they were at home, I would keep walking towards the danger. Foolish it may have seemed, but what mother would not have done the same?

[1] *The Zulu led IFP always had a strong emphasis on representing the Zulu people and their traditions. In the struggle against apartheid this was overshadowed for a time and the IFP and ANC were considered partners in the struggle. However an increasing tension grew between the Parties, as the issue of Zulu identity came back to the fore front of the IFP. Thus during and after the first democratic elections of 1994 the IFP claimed that the ANC did not represent their interests and there were many violent clashes between the two parties. Although since the 1999 elections there has been relative peace between the two.*

Of course I was scared, but more so for my children than for myself. My eyes encountered more and more horrific sights the further I travelled into Ntzuma. There were people lying injured on the road, houses being devoured by flames. I could hear screams of pain in the distance. The more I saw, the more anxious I became, my thoughts running wild. Where were my children? Were they safe? Would I ever see them again? I started to move my feet faster and almost broke into a run as I drew closer to my home, praying that I would find my children there, safe and unharmed.

The door was wide open when I arrived and rushing through it, I called out for my children. But no one answered. There was no one home. I ran into the kitchen and saw the food I had left for dinner, untouched on the table. I collapsed into one of the chairs and lay my forehead on the worktop, trying to steady my breathing. I knew that if I was going to find my children, I would have to remain calm. As my breathing slowed and I collected my thoughts, I decided I could not just sit and wait. I must go out and look for them.

I walked out of the house and saw some people I knew. I asked them if they had seen my children. They had not. They pointed to where a lot of bodies had been piled up, people who had been shot dead in the fighting. My heart sank. I did not believe that my children were dead, but I knew I had to go check.

It was a horrible sight and I can still recall the terrible stench. Bodies were piled up one on top of the other and those still lucky to be alive were walking through them, inspecting each body in turn to see if their loved ones were there. Howls filled the air as upturned bodies revealed familiar but now vacant faces. Like them I began to search, praying all the time that I would not find what I was looking for. I lifted each body, breathing a sigh of relief each time the lifeless face staring back at me was not one of my own.

I finished searching, and while I was no closer to finding my children, at least there was still some hope that they were alive. I went back to my house, thinking that maybe they would have returned home by now. Yet the house was still empty and the food on the table remained untouched. I rested my hands on the worktop. There was little strength left in my body and I had to hold myself up. My legs crumbled beneath me, and again I collapsed over the table.

I do not know how long I sat there. It was getting darker by the minute and I did not know what to do. Every passing minute that they did not return increased my anxiety.

A knock at the window caused me to jump out of my seat. Peering through the darkness I could just about see the outline of someone staring back at me through the glass. When I did not move, they knocked again and shouted through the window, warning me.

'Hey hey, don't sleep in the house, it is not safe! They are burning all the houses!'

With that they were gone. I heard their warning, but I had no choice but to stay put. Where could I go? And what about my children? There was still a chance that they would return and I wanted to be there if they did. So I did all that I knew how to do: I prayed, silently in my heart, as I was too afraid to speak out loud.

'God, I am here by myself,' was the whisper of my heart. 'You know about me and the situation that I am in. I do not know what to do. Please show me the way and protect my children.'

It was now completely dark, and we had no electricity in the house. Yet as I stopped praying, it was as though I could see a little more clearly through the blackness. I looked out of the window, and at that moment I saw two men approaching my house, about to come in the door. Fear brought strength to my feeble body, and I slipped into the living room, where I crawled under the sofa as they entered the house. Lying as still as possible, I made every effort to slow my frantic breathing. I heard them looking through the house. My heart began to beat harder and harder in my chest as I knew any moment they would enter the room where I was hiding.

As I heard their footsteps approaching, I held my breath and squeezed my eyes tight. I waited for them to discover my hiding place, knowing that if they found me I was as good as dead. All I could think about was my children. A mother knows when her children are still alive and I knew that they were out there somewhere. What would happen to them if I were to die now? The men were so close to me and I can still remember the strong smell of alcohol seeping out of their pores. I opened my eyes for a brief moment and saw that their feet were right next to my head.

'Let's burn the place down,' one of them said, his voice cold and detached - hatred driving him to disregard the lives that he was destroying.

'No,' the other replied. His voice carried the same sentiment as his accomplice. 'Look, there is still food on the table. They will come back and when they do we will shoot and kill them.'

I trembled at the sound of their words, but even more so at the hatred in which they were spoken. What had become of my people that we had come to hate each other so much? Why were we so intent on hurting one another? I was lost in the pain of my own thoughts and when I arrived back at my present situation, I realised that the men had left the house. I was relieved momentarily, but knew they would be back.

I stayed under the sofa all night, too scared to move and too scared to sleep, though I managed to find some comfort in the knowledge that my God knew exactly what was going to happen and where my children were. No matter what happened, He had me covered.

It was a long night, but finally the darkness lifted and a new day began to wake. I pulled myself out from under the sofa; how my body ached from lying there all night! I did not waste a moment, not even stopping to wash my face. Still wearing the same clothes from the day before, I grabbed my bag and got out of there. I still did not know what to do about my children, but I knew all I could do was entrust them to God. Wherever they were, they needed a mother who was alive.

I jumped in the first taxi that came by, sitting down next to an auntie I knew.

'Hey,' she asked, 'where is your first born? I saw one of his shoes lying in the street.'

Her words made me feel sick, and the hope I was holding on to with all my might began to dwindle. I did not want to speak to the auntie. I did not want to speak to anyone. With eyes downwards I replied, just loud enough so that she could hear and quiet enough in the hope that she might get the hint and leave me alone.

'I did not see anyone.'

I could not waylay the tears any longer and while I tired hard not to draw any attention to myself, I let them fall silently down my face. By the time I reached my workplace, I could barely put one foot in front of the other. The lady I worked for was a good lady and when I told her what had happened, she said I could use the phone and call anyone I could think of who might be able to help find my children. But I did not call anyone. Who would I call?

Instead my son called me.

'Hello Mama?'

At the sound of his voice, relief washed all over me.

'Are you still alive? What happened? They found your shoe?'

He began to tell me what had happened, how when the shooting started, he fell to the ground and his shoe had fallen off. He only realised later that he had lost a shoe! They had all taken shelter at a friend's house, and thankfully like me they had all made it through the night alive. Thank God they did

We did not go back to Ntzuma for three months. That is how long the fighting lasted. Even then, we only went back to collect what we could. Now I had to find my family a new home. And that's how I came to find myself living here in Burlington.

When we first came here, it was not like it is now. No not at all! It was a nice place – quiet. There were not so many people and far fewer houses than you see now. I thought that it would be a good place for us to live and safer than Ntzuma. Of course I could not know how things were to change. I bought our house from an Indian family and it is the same house that we are living in today, although I have made lots of changes to it over the years. Originally it was a tin house, but now you can see that it is only the roof that is tin. Life was fine and peaceful here for a time and I was lulled into a false sense of comfort that was shattered when in

1997, just as it had in Ntzuma, the fighting began.

I still had the same job, and one day while I was at work I received a phone call. I was surprised that it was for me. It was not often that anyone had to call me at work, you see. Curiously I picked up the receiver and heard my daughter's voice on the other end. She was talking so fast and was in such a panic that I could not make out a word she was saying.

'Slow down, slow down,' I was saying, when a man's voice interrupted hers.

'Come home quickly,' he said, 'your house and children are being shot at!'

Dropping the phone, I left it swinging by the cord and rushed out without even telling my employer that I was leaving. I was frantic the entire journey, wondering what I was going to find when I got home.

As I jumped out of the taxi and ran towards my house, the first thing I saw was that all the windows had been blown out. There was a crowd of people mingling around outside. Pushing past them all, I stepped inside my front door, crunching over the glass underneath my feet. There were empty bullet shells all over the place, seeming to confirm what I feared. There was no way that anyone could have survived such a rampant onslaught.

Yet this was not the case: all my children were present and miraculously unscathed. Not one of them was hurt, not even a scratch! Again my God had protected my children, and no one can deny the miracle that He performed that day.

It was after this that Burlington began to change, seemingly overnight. Something happened that day and it has never been the same again. Some people stayed, but many ran away. Some new people came to replace the ones that had left. Then more and more came, until Burlington was quiet no longer. They began to build new houses and the shacks that you see here today. The more people that came, the more the fighting became commonplace, especially between supporters of the ANC and IFP.

And every week, by the time Sunday came round again, there would be a report of someone dying, the result of some stupid argument or feud. I remember one Sunday, I was on my way to church. I made it half way down the street when I saw that they were burning someone alive. I was so scared that I turned around and ran straight back to my home.

Now it is no better - if anything it is worse! The people that live here are always drinking in the *shebeens* (drinking houses). I don't know what is going on. People against people; they are all trying to kill and destroy one another. These are the things that are happening here now. I hope that one day they will stop, because we are not bad people. All we can do is keep praying and offer help to the needy who come across our path.

You see now that I am older, I no longer work, but I am always busy. There is always someone here that needs help, and I am busier than ever. I am like a mad woman. I run here and I run there. When someone is sick, I go to them and clean their house. If someone is crying, I will go and see what is wrong. Now I have started a soup kitchen at the clinic on a Monday. No one told me to do it and I don't get paid. The people that go to the clinic are sick and get up so early to come that they do not have time to eat. So I thought, 'I must make soup for them'. Every week my daughters, and my grand-daughters too, help me to buy the food to make it. I like to keep myself busy and help people. If I end up with no food, then I end up with no food, but I must share what I do have.

You see, God got hold of me when I was young and He has never let go of me. My life has been interesting. I have seen many things, things that there is not enough time to tell you about right now. But throughout it all, God has never let me down. I know that His hand is upon Burlington and all who live here. And while there is still life in this body I will continue to be His hands and His feet, until the day He takes me home.

Thandazile's Story

The air around me was thick with fear,
Each minute of each hour it became thicker still.
Another day arrived, bringing no news,
And less hope than before.

My eldest brother was missing. And while my mother was trying hard to conceal her increasing anxiety, I knew she was worried. Her eyes, still red from a sleepless night before, stared blankly ahead of her as she sat stiffly on the edge of her seat.

Watching her quietly, I wondered what I could do to make her smile again. Reaching forward I took hold of her hand and feeling my small hand slip into hers, she gently curled up the corners of her mouth, in an attempt at a smile. Young as I was, I was not fooled by her effort to soothe me. I felt the fear emanating from her body, adding to the invisible yet thick cloud invading the air.

I did not know that my brother was never coming home. Nor did I know that his disappearance, along with my father's recent death, would trigger a sequence of events that would change my life forever.

They found his body by the sugar cane field, hanging from a tree with his eyes gouged out. It was a family crime. As the first born of my father's children, my eldest brother stood to inherit that which my father had left behind in death. However, my father had another son; a son not of my mother's womb. His jealousy and greed for our father's money led him to kill his own flesh and blood. Still now I do not know all the details of what happened. What I do know is that after my father and my brother died, life became hard. My mother had to find a job to support the rest of us. Leaving my brother, sister and me at home to fend for ourselves and keep an eye on the farm, she went to look for work in Durban.

Unfortunately, when my mother was away things did not fare so well for the children she left behind.

There was a farmhand who used to come and help us look after the cows. One day my sister and I noticed that he had allowed the cows into the mealie field. My sister ran towards him, while I followed closely behind.

'What are you doing?' she shouted at him, 'Are you crazy? Get those cows out of that field!'

The boy looked up at us, but did nothing to rectify the situation. Instead he simply turned his back on us, dismissing us. My sister was furious, and bending down she picked up a stone. She pulled her arm back, high above her head and aimed the stone in the direction of the boy.

Quickly, before she had a chance to throw it, I reached up and grabbed hold of her arm.

'You can't throw that at him,' I insisted, 'he's a boy and bigger than us!'

Ignoring me and pulling her arm free from mine, she propelled it forward, opening her hand at the last second to send the stone soaring through the air. Time seemed to freeze temporarily as the stone hit his body and I held my breath. His expression of surprise quickly changed to one of anger as he realised what had happened. Time started moving again as he broke into a run, straight for us.

'Come on!' my sister yelled and grabbing hold of my arm, pulled me back towards our house. Running through the door, just in time, we slammed it shut behind us and locked him out. With our backs against the door, we felt him slam into the other side, but he soon realised that he could not get in.

'Don't think I won't get you back for this,' he shouted, 'I'll come back and get you when you least expect it!'

We waited in the house until we were sure he was gone, but we were too scared to stay there alone that night. Just as it was getting dark, we took one last look out of the window and seeing no sign of him, we fled to our neighbour's house. They let us stay that night and every night thereafter, while our mother was away. In the morning we would go back to the farm and check that everything was safe and do our daily chores.

Some time later my brother, sister and I were all on our way home to do just that. As we drew closer we saw smoke coming from the direction of our house. Quickening our pace, my heart stopped as we saw the smoke coming from where our home had once stood.

We broke into a run, but it was already too late. Only a few flames remained, devouring the last of the wood that had once formed our home. Smoke billowed into the sky, indifferent to the pile of ash and devastation it left behind. I fell to my knees and a sudden gust of wind swept past, sending wafts of smoke into my face. The smoke stung my eyes and I lifted my hands to protect them. In doing so, I smeared the tears that were now streaming down my cheeks as I realised all we owned was gone. Slowly we walked back to the neighbour's house, none of us saying a word, all of us wondering what would become of us now.

To this day I do not know who it was that set fire to our home. Perhaps it was the boy who worked on the farm or maybe it was more family members, angry that the farm had been left to us after our father's death. Regardless, it was another blow to our family.

We called our mother from the local shop. And like my mother always did, she took the bad news well.

'Only God knows why these things are happening to us,' she would tell us in such times.

She believed that everything, good or bad, happened for a reason and we had to make the best of it. Not long after that, my mother found a job working as a domestic for an Indian family in Durban. So my sister, my brother and I all moved, and received government housing here in Burlington. My now eldest brother, who had been living away from home, also joined us. Life in Burlington was different from the farm. It was strange having people living so close by, even though there were fewer houses than there are now.

It was a big change, but we adapted quickly, as children do, and soon I went back to school. I had always enjoyed school; I loved learning and dreamed of becoming a social worker. Every day my mother would wake us up early to catch the train. But one morning, I awoke to a dull ache in my head. I began to sit up, but sank back into the bed. Lifting my hand to my head, I called for my mother. Coming close, she felt my forehead and after a moments consideration she decided that I should not go to school. Since she had to go to work, my sister would stay home to look after me. Before she left, she sat down beside us on the bed. Looking us both in the eyes, she desperately tried to get us to listen to her.

'Please my children,' she said, imploring us both. 'Stay in the house. Do not go to the river; for I dreamt that something bad will happen if you do.'

But we did not listen. There were mangos, you see.

On the other side of the river there are mango trees, and that day we wanted mango. So, ignoring our mother's warning and despite my earlier headache, we left the house and made our way down to the river. The river was fierce. Loudly, its waters rushed past, causing us to raise our voices to a shout. Still, we could see the mango trees on the other side and we were determined to pick them.

Cautiously, I began to cross over first, jumping from one stone to the next. I beckoned for my sister to follow. However, the rocks were too slippery for her. Hearing her scream my name I turned around, just in time to see the river pulling her with it. Crouching down I stretched my hand out to catch her, but it was already too late and she was swept past me. A rush of water came up behind me and I too tumbled in.

Terror gripped me as the strength of the waters pulled me under. I struggled and fought my way back to the surface and, taking in great mouthfuls of air, looked around frantically for my sister.

I couldn't see her anywhere.

I managed to grab hold of a rock further down the river and clung to it desperately. Scanning the water, I saw my sister resurface not far from where I was and I screamed her name. Hearing me shout, she looked in my direction and I could see the fear that I felt mirrored in her eyes. I tried to reach for her, but the river was far stronger than either of us and our attempts to battle it were futile.

I could only watch as my sister was swept further and further away from me, till eventually I could see her no more.

That was the last time I saw my sister.

I don't know why, but the river spared me that day. I managed to scramble out of the water and I walked back to our house, water dripping from me as I went. I suddenly remembered that we had left a pot on the stove and I quickened my pace, worrying that it might burn or catch fire. I forgot about my sister momentarily. Blocked it from my mind, afraid of what I might do if I really took in what had just happened.

I don't know who called for help, but it was not me.

The police came, and helicopters too with divers and nets, but they could not find my sister. As time passed I knew that there was little hope that they would find her alive, but even so I continued to hope that she would come back to us.

Two weeks later one of my brothers found her body further down the river.

When my sister died, a part of me died with her. I had never known life apart from her and I grieved for her every day. Tears became my constant companion, and despite my mother's best efforts to help me get back to normal, I knew that things would never be the same again.

However, life was not patient with me and it continued to play out despite my reluctance to join in. Each new day determined to turn into the next, until on one not so particularly special day, tragedy struck my family yet again.

Burlington was turning more and more violent as the people in the community started fighting against each other. It was becoming common place for violence to erupt at a moment's notice and for gunshots to be heard while we sat at home eating our supper. So far we had escaped unscathed, though it was not to remain that way. You see, my eldest brother was an avid supporter of the ANC (African National Congress). He attended all the rallies, had the flag and followed them whole-heartedly. However, there were people here in Burlington who did not like this and they were about to let us know exactly how they felt.

It was well into the evening the night that it happened. I was busy with my homework when my auntie asked me to go and make the tea. I put my pencil down, pushed my chair back from the table and made my way to the kitchen. My friend Zinhle was visiting and she followed me out of the room to help.

I was putting the pot of water on the stove to boil, when Zinhle came near and very quietly, close to my ear, said, 'There are some men standing out there.' She pointed to a spot just outside of the window. A slight tremor in her voice revealed her anxiety, but I shrugged it off.

'It's ok,' I said, 'people often pass by there.'

I didn't know how wrong I was.

Suddenly the kitchen flooded with darkness as the lights failed and before I had a chance to move, I heard a loud bang. It was so close that my whole body trembled. I had heard enough to know that it was a gunshot and grabbing Zinhle, I pulled her down with me onto the ground. My heart was pounding in my chest. There was another shot and then another. Without saying a word, Zinhle and I ran off, she in one direction heading for safety and I in the other to warn my family.

I knew that it was too late for my eldest brother as the gunmen had approached his room first, but there was still hope for the others. Running to the window of the room I had just left, I shouted at them.

'Close the door!'

Hearing the door close and knowing that they were at least safe, I slid down the wall of the house until I was crouching on the ground, wordlessly praying that I would remain hidden there in the dark.

Unfortunately I did not.

Before long I sensed movement close by and peering into the darkness I could see the vague outline of a man walking towards me. He held a gun almost casually by his side and as he approached I looked up into the dark sky and cried, 'Oh God, if it's my day to die then take me quickly, if not then please save me!'

Clambering to my feet I started to run, but it was no use. The man was already too close. There was no chance of escape.
I watched as he raised his arm and, aiming the gun in my direction, pulled the trigger. Squeezing my eyes shut, I braced myself for the inevitable. As the bullet hit my leg, I fell to the ground and the agony of it momentarily replaced my fear. Though it quickly returned when I heard the gunman coming even closer.

Looking up, I saw him looking straight back down at me. The light cast from the moon revealed his face. It was void of any emotion as he leaned over and squatting down next to me, forcibly pushed the gun into my side. He was so close that I felt his breath on my cheek as he pulled the trigger again and again, pumping four more bullets into my body.

The pain tore through me as the man stood up and walked into the dark night. As the sound of his footsteps disappeared, all I could do was wonder how long it would take for me to die.

I don't know how long I lay there. It couldn't have been all that long, but time was irrelevant as the pain quickly consumed every part of me.

It was my mother who found me. Waiting as long as she could bear after the gunshots had ceased, she had rushed out in search of me and my brother. She immediately hurried off to get help, but before she came back I felt another presence by my side. I felt someone touch me and heard a voice exclaiming, 'Ah Thanda, you are still alive!' At first I could not place the voice, and then I recognised it as my neighbour's. My mother returned at that moment, frantic and unable to call for an ambulance as all the phone lines had been cut. Thankfully my neighbour was able to find a car and they drove me to the hospital.

I do not remember much of that journey, as I lapsed in and out of consciousness. The pain remained, but I became strangely detached from it as the shock of what had happened took over. At the hospital my injured body was transferred to a hospital gurney and I was rushed into the emergency room. There was increasing commotion and activity around me and although I was aware of it, it seemed to get quieter rather than louder. Eventually I did not have the strength to keep my eyes open and I allowed the darkness to take over.

When I awoke again, I found myself in a dimly lit room. For a moment I did not remember what had happened and then it all came flooding back to me. I could hear the rhythmic beep of the machines attached to my body and something else. Slowly I recognised it as the sound of someone quietly sobbing. I tried to turn to find out who it was, but my body did not respond to my instructions. I was unable to move at all. The only part of me that I could move was my eyes and as I did I caught sight of my mother sitting by the bed where I lay.

It was she who was sobbing, her body hunched over the bed, her head resting upon my hand which she held in both of her own. She was earnestly whispering something over and over again and I strained to hear what it was. I wished that the noise of the machines - busy working to keep me alive, would be quiet for a moment so that I could hear. Eventually I made out the words she was uttering.

'Please don't die, Thanda,' she pleaded, 'please don't die!'

I tried to speak, but there was a tube down my throat, helping me to breathe. There was nothing that I could do to reassure her, though I desperately wanted to let her know that I was going to live! For in that moment I knew that I would.

Though I would not die, I would not walk again and I have been confined to a wheelchair ever since. It took three years in hospital recovering and learning how to live with my disability before I could return to my mother and brother in Burlington, my only remaining family members. For while I survived the shooting that day, my eldest brother did not.

I lay in my hospital bed and silently mourned him for many days, angry that I did not get the chance to say goodbye. But my anger soon turned into determination to work hard and return home to my mother. Over time I was able to move my upper body again and the day that I had enough strength in my arms to wheel myself to the telephone and call my mother was a major milestone. It was not long after this that I was able to go home.

Burlington was shocked to see me return. Many thought that I had died along with my brother that day and my sudden return sparked a multitude of questions. I returned a different person, inside and out. Of course I was not the only one to have changed. People had moved on; my friends had grown up and while they still came by to visit, there was no denying that things were different. I could no longer do the things I used to do nor have the friends I used to have. And since my house is situated at the bottom of a steep and precarious hill, I soon discovered that I was a prisoner in my own home.

Yet, as I had already experienced, life refused to stop moving. Not even long enough for me to catch a breath. I continued to grow up, developing desires just like any other young teenage girl. And, as every teenage girl almost always does, one day I met a boy.

His name was Simpiwe and he used to visit me when my mother was at work and I was home alone. I thought nothing of it – at first. But then one day he surprised me, when he told me that he loved me.

My first response was to laugh; I was convinced that he was teasing me. After all, I thought, what man could love me in this wheelchair? Yet as the sound of my laughter reached his ears, a look of disappointment came over his face. Seeing this, I quickly slapped a hand over my mouth, making sure that no more laughter could escape. He said no more about it that day and left soon after.

I could not stop thinking about it after he had gone. I had never thought to consider him that way and the idea of a man liking me was a whole new concept. I wondered if he would come back, though I did not have to wait long to find out. A few days later he returned to continue the pursuit.

I don't know when I fell in love with him, but I did.
I didn't know that he would break my heart, but he did.

I was nineteen when I discovered that I was pregnant. It was a big shock. I was convinced that I was unable to have children after being shot and Simpiwe and I had only been together one time! So sure of its impossibility, I had no idea that I was even pregnant at first. Then one day I felt the movement of my unborn child inside my tummy, and I knew.

I told Simpiwe straight away and his first reaction was to run. He returned to his parent's farm, leaving me behind, afraid and all alone. I was so afraid, that I could not bring myself to tell anyone else and for the rest of the pregnancy it remained my secret. Simpiwe was the first and the last person that I told.

It was not as hard as you might think to keep it hidden. My mother was so unsuspecting that any changes in my body went unnoticed. Besides I was not very big – in fact I hardly showed at all. I made sure to rise early and dress (always choosing baggy clothes) before my mother was ready to help me. I shocked my mother with my apparent newfound independence.

'Hau Thanda,' she'd say, 'are you doing things for yourself now?'

'Just because I am in this wheelchair Ma, does not mean that I cannot do things for myself,' I would reply, with mock indignation.

Then at night while sleeping in the same bed, I kept my back to her, curling my body protectively around my growing belly. I loved that child even then. Of course the day eventually came when my child was ready to be born and I could hide it no longer.

The labour pains started and still I could not bring myself to speak. I had kept quiet for so long that I did not know of any words to give voice to what I had been hiding. And to some degree I had convinced myself that it was not real. But real it was, and nothing was going to stop my baby from entering the world.

My mother noticed that something was ailing me, but I assured her that it was only an upset stomach and she was busy in the kitchen when the baby finally decided to come. When the head started to appear, I still had my underwear on and had to cut my panties off with a pair of scissors so that the baby could come out. Walking back into the room where I was, my mother had her first impromptu introduction to her new grand-daughter as she lay crying fervently on the bed.

She said nothing. Instead, she calmly looked at the newborn baby lying on the bed, then back to me and, leaving me to wonder what she was going to do, she turned and walked straight back out of the door. She returned shortly afterwards, having gone to fetch an auntie from up top. They cut the baby's cord and cleaned her up, all the while saying nothing. However, unlike her daughter, my mother could not stay silent for long, and when she finally spoke, she wanted answers.

I told her that Simpiwe was the father and so she called to let him know that his daughter had been born. I am sure he had been waiting anxiously for that phone call, not with concern for me or his child, but in anticipation of my mother's wrath, whose reputation preceded her.

He arrived with clothes for the baby, perhaps hoping the gesture might soften my mother's anger. I am sure that it did not, and my mother did not waste any time letting her feelings be known. As soon as he put his foot in the doorway, she asked, 'Did you take my daughter's virginity?'

With eyes lowered Simpiwe replied, 'Yes Ma, I'm sorry, it was me.'

My mother told him that he must pay *lobola* (bride price). But Simpiwe did not have the money. Of course he assured my mother that he would, and that when that day came he would undoubtedly take me as his wife. I could not help but think back to the very beginning when he had made similar promises to marry me. My doubts about Simpiwe began that day, as I thought that maybe what Simpiwe said and what Simpiwe did were two very different things.

While my mother was angry about what I had done, she was even more angry that I had kept quiet about it.

'Why did you not tell me?' she exclaimed, 'Anything could have happened to you!'

I had no answer for her and simply shrugged my shoulders in response. She sighed deeply, wondering, I presume, what she had done to deserve such a daughter.

Yet my mother was a good woman and I knew that she loved me deeply. As she loved her new grand-daughter. She named her Sindisiwe, meaning healed; a living testament to the miracle of my body being able to carry a child. From then on my mother looked after us both, until the time came when she herself was too sick to do so. I did not realise when they took her to the hospital that it would be the last time I would see her alive. If I had known, I would have told her how much I loved her and how much I was going to miss her. I hope in her heart that she knew.

When she died, a deep darkness descended on my life. I dreaded the morning light and I could not see past my grief. I did nothing to fight it and had neither the strength nor the inclination to pull myself out of it. I could not understand why I was still alive, why God would keep the breath in my body when all I had known was suffering? The pain of all my losses beset me day and night and my heart struggled to survive. There seemed little in my life to live for. If it were not for my daughter Sindi and the discovery that I was going to have another child, I may have given up on life all together.

I prayed that it would be a boy. You see, Simpiwe had made it quite clear that he would leave me if I did not provide him with a son.

'If you have a boy, then I will marry you and I will love you forever,' he said. 'But if you have a girl, then I must cheat on you. I must find someone else who can give me what I want.'

Throughout the pregnancy I was worried, knowing that the future of my relationship depended on the sex of the child growing inside of me. But there was nothing that I could do but wait and pray, which I did with all of my might. Day and night I pleaded with God.

'Dear God will you do me a favour?' I asked. 'Could you give me a boy?'

But there was no way of knowing whether God would see fit to answer me favourably until the baby was born. Yet despite my anxiety, my love was unconditional and as my child grew in my tummy, so did the love in my heart, waging war against the pain and the loss that had taken residence over the years.

God heard my prayers and my new son was a gift from above, which is why I named him Sipho (gift). For despite my worsening circumstances, the birth of my children brought with it a love that forced me to keep going. It is a mother's love; the same love that my mother had for me. It gave her the strength to push through the hard times, and just as she had lived for me and my siblings I would live for my own children, giving them the life that my mother had tried so hard to give me.

The arrival of my son did not take away all my insecurities about Simpiwe and as I had suspected years before, Simpiwe was not a man who held true to his word. I waited for him to come back from work with money for the child, but he never came. I did not need to be told where he was and despite his later denial I knew what he had been up to. I had discovered that he was looking for love in the arms of another. This was something that I would not stand for and I reminded Simpiwe of the second name that we had given our son.

'You wanted a boy, I gave you a boy and you said that you would never cheat! What is your child's name? It is Kwanele – enough! I have had enough – now you must leave. Now you have no child.'

I have never gone back on my word.

Since then it has just been me and my kids, and it is my love for them that has pulled me through; a love which I have learned comes from God above. Somehow, somewhere, He has connected with my heart, pushing aside the pain of the past and giving me the strength to let go. He has sent people into my life who have pointed me towards Him and helped me make sense of my life. Now He has given me joy that I can never remember having before, not even as a child. I want others to have that joy too, especially the people in Burlington. I see them here, lost and

Zuziwe's Story

Lies and secrets, things left untold,
Are the only certainties my life has ever known.
And while I've tried hard to figure it all out,
I'm still not sure what is really going on.

The truth always has a way of coming out in the end. Pushing itself to the surface; urging those holding the key to set it free. However, I have discovered that once a lie has been told, people will try and hold on to it no matter what the cost. And while I have uncovered many of the lies spoken over my life, there still could be more that I am not aware of.

My name is Zuziwe and I am going to tell you my story so far. Not that I have found all the answers: those are what I am still looking for. Maybe in the telling of my story I will stumble across them; perhaps they are just waiting to be found.

I was thirty years old when I discovered that I was not my mother's daughter; that the woman who had brought me up and whom I had called mother, was actually my aunt. Suddenly no one was who I thought they were. I was not who I thought I was. Everything I held to be true in my life was actually a lie.

Yet at least now some things made sense. I remembered little things; things I should have paid more attention to, as they hinted towards my true identity and where I really belonged.

There were the times when my 'supposed' brother returned home after spending the month working in Durban. Seeing him approach from afar we would all wait eagerly, wondering what he had brought home for us. Silently I would hope that this time he had remembered me.

He never did. I realise now that he never considered me to be one of them.

'She is not my child; she's yours!' was his standard reply when questioned why he had forgotten me yet again. Unlike me, he knew the truth of who I was. I think I was the only one left in the dark. Although deep down, I always knew something was wrong. I never felt that I truly belonged, although I never knew that was the truth. The feeling was always there, clinging to me before I was even born. As soon as I was conceived in my mother's womb, she did not want me. In fact she wanted to abort me. Only God knows why she didn't.

While I thought that I had always lived there, in reality I only went to live with my aunt when I was fourteen months old. My state at that time spoke volumes of my mother's disregard for my life. I can only assume that my mother had finally had enough of me, although I doubt I will ever know what she truly felt or thought at the time; she never has given me any straight answers. All I know is that my aunt took me in: sick, neglected, my stomach swollen. I do not know whether it was out of choice or not.

Everybody knew the truth except for me,

The neighbours knew.
The teachers knew.
Maybe somewhere buried deep in my subconscious I also knew.

It was a truth unspoken,
A secret festering underneath.
Yet the problem with secrets is –
They are simply too hard to keep.

I was not a bad child, but like all children, at times I did some mischievous things. One day I wanted some bread and I saw money on top of the table. I looked around me cautiously, saw that no one was nearby or watching and quickly snatched the few coins from the table.

I darted out of the house and made my way to the small tuck shop nearby. I bought some bread and wasted no time getting stuck in. Yet while certain things in my life went unnoticed and unaddressed, this was not one of them.

My aunt was quick to discover my thievery and even quicker to discipline me for it. Before I could finish the bread she had caught up with me. I did not see her coming, as I was too engrossed in filling my tummy. She grabbed me by the shirt, the bread falling from my hands and pulled me roughly all the way back to the house. Once there she let loose and hit me so hard, I never dared do it again.

I knew what I had done was wrong, but it did not stop me feeling sorry for myself. I went to my neighbour's house. I suppose I was looking for some sympathy. All I wanted was someone to dry my tears, but I got more than that when my neighbour decided to let me in on some of the neighbourhood secrets … surrounding me!

'She would never have beaten you so hard,' she said as though she were talking about something quite insignificant, 'if you were her real daughter!'

The words startled me out of my self-pity and my tears stopped in mid flow. I looked up at my neighbour, shocked into silence. She said no more after that. I do not know whether it just slipped out or she intentionally told me. I did not wait to find out.

I ran home, straight to my aunt. She said that my neighbour was a liar and assured me that she was my mother. I knew someone was lying to me: unfortunately I did not know who. I chose to believe my aunt that day. You see, I wanted to believe her, whether it were true or not. But I never could get rid of that nagging feeling afterwards, that maybe there was some truth to my neighbour's words.

For while I so desperately wanted to belong, I never truly felt that I did.

I did not really understand what was happening the day that I lost my virginity. Nor was it something that I consented to, or even knew that I could dissent. I was only twelve years old, immature in every way. He was fifteen and why he did it I'll never know. It was after school and we were all alone in the class. There was no one around to protect me. There never was and never has been since. I suppose he knew it and took what he knew he could. Afterwards with tears streaming down my face I cried, 'You took my virginity!' He looked at me as if I were nothing, confirming his thoughts by spitting on me in response.

I saw the look of disgust in his eyes and it added to my own increasing sense of self loathing. Turning away from his stare, I looked out of the window. The sun was bright in my eyes, blinding me with its light. I only wished that it could blind me from the vivid pictures that were repeatedly flashing in my mind.

But I knew that it couldn't.

I ran to the river and immersed myself in its waters, hoping that when I resurfaced I would have washed myself clean. But as I came up for breath, wondering if I had stayed under long enough, I could still feel his filthy hands all over me. I started to scrub my body, so hard that it hurt. I wished that I could scrub away the awful feelings and memories in my head.

But I knew that I couldn't.

The next time it happened I was still only thirteen. This time it was in the bush and though it was a different boy, the way it made me feel was much the same.

But this time I fell pregnant.

I did not know that I was pregnant at first. I was so young. Yet I knew something was happening, as my stomach started to get bigger and I felt something moving inside. I went to my aunt and showed her my stomach. She hadn't noticed up till then and her shock mixed with anger was frightening. She wanted to know who had taken my virginity and on telling her, she went straight to his house.

But the boy denied it, and it was his word against mine.

My son was eight years old when I took him to live with his father. He still tried to deny him, but the likeness was too great for anyone to continue believing him. They finally accepted him and while I did not want to let him go, I had to do what was best for him. You see, I did not have money to take care of him and while he had been the first to give me a child, he was not the last. I had other mouths at home that I could barely feed.

I missed my son terribly when he was gone, but when I took him to live with his father, I knew that it would be difficult to see him again. His father filled me with fear and I was scared that he would beat me, even kill me, if I came anywhere near. I used to visit him at school instead, but I could never see him for long.

I hated not having him with me,
And constantly cried at the loss,
But even when the tears were not falling down my face,
In my heart the weeping never stopped.

I hope my son knew how much I loved him and that I was only doing what I thought was best. And while we could not be together, I prayed every day he would know that his home was deep in my heart and that he would always belong there.

It was in my own search for belonging that I unearthed some more family secrets. The unveiling of this secret came in the form of a letter.

I was visiting my grandfather's house and I found the letter in my sister's room. I could not believe what I read and immediately took it to the neighbour's house, my mother's cousin.

'What have you done?' she exclaimed when I showed her the letter.

'But see!' I replied, 'My brother made my sister pregnant! He took her virginity!'

I don't know what I thought they would do when I told them, but I think in the end it only caused my family to hate me even more. Particularly my brother. He wanted to kill me, though he denied the contents of the letter. However, I think his actions spoke of the truth. Still now I think he would kill me if he knew where I was.

I tried to tell my mother too, but she did not have ears to hear it. She loved my brother and sister so much. As for me, she always hated me when I told the truth; she would rather live a lie. She would rather pretend that everything was well, rather have us all wearing smiles on our faces like a perfect happy family. Yet all the time underneath the ugly truth remained.

Still now they are living the lie. And while others may not know, I know and God knows.

Perhaps it was this, my search for truth that caused my mother to reject me. Perhaps if I had accepted the lies, she would have welcomed me home with loving arms. But while they can live this way, I cannot live their lies.

After this, I gave up on my family and came to Durban in search of a different one.

I did not know anyone in Durban when I first arrived and until I found the home that I was looking for, I lived on the streets. I survived as best as I could, finding shelter in vacated doorways and rummaging for food in the bins. However it was not a life that I could keep on living, and one day I found myself praying.

'Please God,' I prayed, eyes searching the sky, pleading with the One unseen, 'give me a man to take care of me!'

I don't know whether it was God or not, but that very same day I met the old man. He was sitting in a bar, drinking a beer with his friend. I noticed him straight away, but I did not think that he would notice me.

'Hey Sisi,' he said and motioned for me to come over. I did not think twice about whether to respond, though I was a little nervous as I approached his table. As I walked towards him, my eyes travelled from the floor to the old man several times, unsure if I should meet his eyes. However, I need not have worried as I did not have to wait long to discover his intentions.

'I want you to come home with me,' he said. 'I want to make you my wife!'

'Ok,' I replied.

So that same day, same time, I went with him and that is how I came to live here in Burlington, in this very house.

A short while later he sent me back to my aunt's to fetch my children.

'Finally,' I thought, 'I have found them a home!'

He even paid my aunt some *lobola* (bride price): now my children had a father and I was a proper wife! I wanted it so badly, I chose to ignore the obvious fact that he was sick.

My husband was a better man than I had ever known. He told me that he loved me and in the end he proved that he did. All other men had used me and left me; it had been that way since I was a little girl. But unlike them, he looked after me and my children. If I was sick, he supported me and if my children wanted to go to school, he paid the school fees. It was the first time that I felt accepted and cared for, and for the few years that I was with him I actually felt secure.

People may look at my life, see that I have seven children by seven different fathers and make assumptions about who I am. Many call me a prostitute, and do not wait to find out if it is true. But all

Khanyisile's Story

I wonder how many promises are made? And how many promises are broken? How many people are waiting for their dreams to come true, dependent on another person?

I waited for a long time. I did not know that I would. I was so sure in the beginning that I would live the life that I had always dreamt of, and while in my heart I always hoped and never quite gave up, as the years passed by and promises made were constantly broken, my expectations slowly died.

I met Musa when I was in Standard Nine. I was the quiet studious girl, he was the popular boy. Many of the girls liked him, but he chose me.

I suppose at the time I was flattered. We used to talk for hours, yet try as I might I cannot remember what about. I thought we were in love, although now I admit I did not know what love was. But I did not know then what I am telling you now and how it was all going to end.

I told no one about us. It is not the way it is done in my culture, you see. In my culture, if a man is interested in a girl, the proper thing to do is to first approach the parents and let them know. Then if they are looking to marry he must pay *lobola* (bride price). Only then will she leave the home of her father and become his wife. Yet for the most part that is not how it happens these days; and it is not how it happened for me or my sisters.

There are five girls in my family, of which I am the youngest. To the disappointment of our mother, all of us found ourselves pregnant outside of marriage. Only two were lucky enough to have the father of our children do right, by firstly paying *inhlawulo* (damages for impregnation); and then paying *lobola*, to make her a respectable wife. I thought it would happen for me this way; unfortunately it was not to be.

I knew what I was doing was not good; I knew that it was not the right way, but still I did it anyway. I thought that it would be ok. While I had kept our relationship quiet for so long, when I gave Musa my virginity I knew that I had to tell my mother. Virginity is such a precious thing and my mother always told me that if a man ever touched us (be it consensual or not) we must tell her straight away. And while I told her some things and not others, I knew that I had to tell her this.

My mother went straight to Musa's house, wasting no time. She considered it a matter of utmost importance. I can only imagine how she felt when I told her, as I was the fifth of her daughters to go against our traditions and enter into such a relationship before marriage. Later Musa would vent his anger at me, annoyed that I had told my mother about us and worse still, for not telling him that she was on her way to his house. But first he had to face the wrath of his own mother.

And his mother was certainly angry, although not surprised. Her unruly son was often in trouble of some sort and she was used to receiving mothers on her doorstep with charges against him. I guess she knew that it was only a matter of time before it would be trouble of this sort. She was a good woman and always did what was right, and so Musa was made to leave school straight away and start working both to pay back our family for his mistake and also to earn enough money for *lobola*.

Of course, I was told not to see him after this. My mother was quite insistent, but other than removing me from school, there was little that she could do to curb our relationship. I should have listened to her, but I thought I knew best; what teenage girl doesn't? Anyway, I was sure that Musa was going to pay *lobola* and while falling pregnant was not part of the plan, I assumed it only served to confirm that I would soon be his wife.

I had not known I was pregnant at first. The thought had not even entered my head. Stupidly I thought that it wouldn't happen to me. It might be what they all say, but it is also very true. We choose to ignore that nagging sense deep in the pit of our stomach, telling us to be careful, until it is much too late.

I thought for a long time about the best way to break it to my mother. I tried to think of words that would make it easier for her to hear, but I soon realised that there were none. She did not say much when I told her. I think that she had used up all her words on my sisters in the same predicament years earlier. Besides, my mother was not like many other mothers. She was not one to shout and scream. Although I think if she had, it might have made me feel better, for the look on her face was worse than any words she could have uttered. The look of total disappointment broke my heart.

Still, I was sure that Musa would marry me and everything was going to be alright. I daydreamed about building our own home, where we would bring up our children together, just like my mother and father had.

'It was your father's sisters who spotted me first,' my mother often told us, fondly reminiscing over times gone by. 'They liked the look of me and thinking I would make a suitable wife for their brother, told him to go and observe me by the river.'

In those days, a man would go and watch the girls as they fetched water from the river. My mother was told that my father would be coming by, and watching as he and his friend approached, she made a quick decision.

'If it is the one walking on the right,' she thought, 'then I shall say yes. But if it is the other, it will definitely be a no!' Fortunately for my father, he was the one walking on the right.

I loved hearing my mother talk about my father. I could hear the affection in her voice and see the tenderness in her eyes as she recalled the years they had spent together. Theirs was a marriage unlike others, and my mother had no sympathy with all the problems the other women complained about; husbands who cheated on them, who didn't bring home any money, who drank all their wages away. I think some of the women who lived nearby were jealous of the good man that she had secured, and they did not make it easy for her.

Yet even her fairytale did not have the happiest of endings, for when I was ten years old my father died. While I know now that my mother must have been deeply affected by this, she never showed her grief to us children. She had a quiet strength and battled on through it alone. She was still young enough to marry again, but she never did. In later years she told me that there was only one man for her and she did not have any inclination to marry again.

Hearing my mother talk, I longed for that same kind of love. I realise now that I should have waited for my husband to come to me, for him to pursue me properly instead of rushing in with my heart. But by doing it my way, and being secretive in the process, I gave up the counsel of those wiser than myself. I did not choose my man well.

As with many other things in my life, I kept quiet about my pregnancy to all but my immediate family. Outside our home I did everything to hide my growing belly. I wore baggier clothes as the months went by, borrowing my mother's jumpers. I felt the shame of my situation fall heavy upon me, the shame becoming heavier and heavier each day that Musa did not pay. And while my mother stayed quiet on the subject, my other family members did not. They never grew weary of telling me how stupid I had been and reminded me day and night about the shame I had brought on the whole family. There was nothing that I could do but endure it.

I continued with my schooling, as it was an important year for me with my matric (final year). I was a good student and my plans were to go on to university and make something of my life. It was something my father had wanted for all his children, even us girls. Fortunately no one at school caught on that I was pregnant. I was a good and quiet student and none of my teachers or classmates suspected me. They merely assumed I was gaining some weight, and I did nothing to suggest otherwise. However, my baby was due before my final exams and my secret was to be made public before I had the chance to sit them.

I had to have a caesarean, but I was not worried about that. I was more concerned about my exams. My education was the only thing that I had any control over and I was determined to take hold of this part of my life. Unfortunately the school noticed my absence and called my mother to find out where I was. When she told them that I was in hospital giving birth to a child, they told her I need not bother coming back.

It was worse than finding out I was pregnant in the first place, and it was the final blow in what was becoming the worst year of my young life. My life was falling apart around me and there was nothing that I could do to bring the pieces of it back together, no matter how much I tried.

I berated myself for being so stupid. Looking at my new-born baby boy, I could only see him as a hindrance to my future. Deep down I knew that it was not his fault, but I could not stop the negative thoughts from entering my head.

'If only he was not here,' I thought, 'then I'd be able to write my exams and get on with my education!'

Sometimes, I felt so much anger towards my son, simply for being born. Then, in the next moment, I was full of guilt, knowing that it was not his fault. Motherhood, I discovered, was not easy and yet I could not stop the love from creeping in. It took hold of me and my son became the object of all my affection.

My mother taught me how to care for him, helping to awake the mothering instincts inside of me. Gentle in her instruction, she had a way that never made me feel inadequate or stupid. And in years to come, as my son grew physically, she supported me as much as she could. I understood the shame that I had brought upon the family, but unlike the rest of my relatives she did not continually remind me of it.

Yet I could not forget it. Whether it was talked about or not, it was always there and the longer Musa failed to make amends the worse it got. Soon the anger I had initially felt towards my son was transferred towards Musa.

It was Musa who named our son Sthembiso (promise). He said that it was a reminder of his promise to me - the promise of a life spent together. In the beginning I thought that he would fulfil his promise, and at first he did bring home money to support us, having secured a job in Durban. But as time passed I could not bear the waiting, until eventually I did not want to see him at all. I no longer wanted to hear his empty words; words promising me that now he was working he would soon make things right. But words are too easy to say: they are much harder to live up to. I wanted to see him actually follow through on something! In the end, the name of our son did not make me hopeful, but only reminded me of his father's unfulfilled promises. I determined never to let him touch me again.

So I decided to get on with my own life as best as I could. Whilst my dreams for a life with Musa as his wife slipped further and further away, I still clung to my desires for an education and to accomplish something good with my life. So when my son was three years old, I went to college in Durban to finish my schooling.

While at school, I stayed in Umlazi, a bigger township here in Durban. I worked hard that year and the hard work paid off, as I got good grades in my final exams. At last, I thought I had finally got them, if a little late, and now I was all set to go to university. However, my dreams crashed again when my mother told me that there was no longer enough money for this.

It seemed as though whenever my dreams were within reach, something happened to push them further away. All my hard work now seemed pointless, and I wondered why I had even tried. My future stretched out before me and I could see nothing good in it. Disappointed and upset, I decided to join my sister in Hammersdale rather than go home. I found myself a job in the Chatsworth area and settled myself into it.

I was unaware of what was just around the corner.

On my way home one day, I passed a group of men returning from a football game. They were in jovial mood, and there were the usual comments as I walked past. 'Khanyisile!' I heard, and looking up from the pavement where I had fixed my gaze, I found myself face to face with Musa.

As surprised as I was to see him, he too was shocked to see me in Durban, but at the same time he appeared delighted. I was taken aback at bumping into him so randomly, but also by his eager behaviour towards me. He introduced me to his friends as his wife, and while I liked hearing such words coming out of his mouth, I was quick to correct him. It would have been nice to pretend for a little while that it was true, but there was no denying that it wasn't. I too was happy to see him: though I had tried hard to conceal it and as much as I wanted to hate him, I never could.

'Come see where I live,' he said, and against my better judgement I agreed, accompanying him here to his house in Burlington. I often wonder how things would have turned out if I hadn't. I had been scared of what might occur between us if I didn't stay away from him. And in the end I had been right to stay away, as I soon found myself pregnant with my second child.

As usual Musa did not take it seriously. Everything was always a big joke to him and this was no different. However, I did not see it that way and neither did my mother. In her usual few words she told me what I was doing was not good, reminding me that I was supposed to be working to get enough money to go to university, not having another child. It was not something I needed to be reminded of, but we both knew that she was right.

Unlike with my first pregnancy, Musa was now working and he was able to support me more this time, so things were a little better during my second pregnancy. It stirred the hope inside of me that maybe he would get his act together and finally make me his wife. But my hope was short-lived, for when my son Iyanda was born, everything changed.

I don't know exactly what changed him; I can only guess. I think that it was in part the pressure of now having two sons and having to support them both; yet more than that I think that it was Burlington itself. I see the way that people can be here. No one seems to care for themselves, never mind for each other. As for the girls, they tend to throw themselves at the men and from what I have seen, the men rarely say no. Musa was no different.

I did not know it at first, but Musa had many girlfriends here in Burlington. But it was not until after Iyanda was born that I found out about them. I suppose I was stupid to think that there was only me, but I was young and still hopeful.

He used to call me to bring the kids to see him and to collect the money for their support. In the beginning I always went. On one such occasion I was not there long when I noticed a pile of baby napkins sitting by the door. Picking one up from the pile, I walked over to where Musa sat idly watching the TV.

'Whose are these?' I asked pushing it in front of his face. He looked at the napkin in my hand.

'Oh those? My third's son's mother left them here,' he said quickly.

Silence ensued for a few moments. His revelation hung heavy in the air, and while he may not have considered it significant, the change in atmosphere told a different story. A massive argument followed, bigger than any we'd ever had before. He spoke as though I already knew about his other children, and not as though I were hearing it for the first time. Still, he never quite looked me in the eye. He also had another child in between my two sons. A little girl, born to a woman I had gone to school with. I guess that when I had refused to let him touch me after I found out that I was pregnant, he went elsewhere. In the end I left, resolving to never again come running when he beckoned.

'You know where your sons are,' I said. 'When you feel fit to support them, you can bring the money to us!'

Turning my back on him, I walked out of his house, determined to rid my heart of him once and for all. Later when the anger subsided, I would cry over his blatant disregard for me and his sons. But in that moment I refused to let him see how much he had hurt me.

By this time my sister and I were also living in Burlington, so it was hard to avoid Musa. Neither did he make it easy for me. Now that I had stood up for myself, he chased me all the time. He was always troubling me, saying he was sorry, but doing nothing to prove it.

I decided to prove to him that it was over.

I found myself another boyfriend. I thought that it would help me get over Musa, but nothing I did seemed to stop the pull towards him. Even worse than that, I found it hard to trust another man. So in the end I broke up with my boyfriend. It seemed my heart and my mind were at war; in my mind I knew that it was fruitless to keep thinking Musa was ever going to change, but in my heart I could not stop hoping.

I was happy when the factory I worked for moved to Pietermaritzburg and I was given the chance to move along with it. Perhaps with some distance between Musa and myself, my heart might finally recover. I tried to help it along by finding myself another boyfriend. After all, I thought, all the other girls were doing it and my family was not around to say anything. Still it went against all the values I had been brought up with, and while I prided myself in only having one boyfriend at a time, it was not good for me.

Time after time my relationships ended. Despite the physical distance I had put between myself and Musa, I could not seem to distance myself from him in my heart. At times I would have enough of men all together and stay single!

But my decision did not sit well with the other women I worked and lived with. They seemed to think that it was very much their business and not just mine. I am not entirely sure why they found it such a problem, but I can guess. I think they feared that if I did not have a man of my own, I would go after theirs. They could not understand that I did not want a man at all, and certainly did not want one of theirs! They were rarely single, often having more than one boyfriend at a time to meet all of their needs. As for me, I seemed to get along better without one.

I did not enjoy being the focus of their discussions. I saw their looks and heard their whispers.

'Why does she not have a boyfriend?' I would hear them ask one another, just loud enough so I could hear. 'Is there nobody who is interested in her? Is she not attractive or what?'

Eventually all the talking would get to me and I would give in to the constant voices telling me that it was not normal for a young woman to be single and alone. I would spy out a man, one who looked good, one who talked good.

'Maybe this one will be the right one!' I would think. He never was.

I had been in Pietermaritzburg less than a year when I received a phone call that changed everything. My mother had taken ill and I was told to return home as quickly as possible. It was not a massive shock. You see, my mother had been ill for quite some time. She'd had a stroke a few years earlier and had never been the same since, and while the love for her family never left, many of her other basic senses did. She became much like a child and needed constant care. She lost a lot of her memory and often would be caught wandering away from the house, on her way to visit a friend who had died many years before. I hated seeing her this way: we all did. So when the news came that she was close to death, I thought that God was finally taking her to rest and to be reunited with my father.

I went home straight away and coming into view of our family house, the first thing that I saw was the funeral services parked outside. The sight caused me to quicken my pace, although I am not sure why now, for its presence told me it was already too late. By the time I reached the front door, they were carrying my mother's body out.

We all know that death is certain, but even when we know it is close and indeed that it is better for the one suffering in life to pass, there is nothing that can truly prepare us for it and the void their passing leaves in our lives. My mother was the backbone of our family. Even during the years after her stroke, the strength that emanated from her presence held our family together. Now she was gone.

When someone dies, it either pulls a family closer together or pushes them further apart. It was the latter that occurred in my family. We stopped acting like a family. Instead everybody looked out for themselves and for the most part ignored the troubles of the others.

I decided to move home, but struggled to find a job, although my younger brother helped me out where he could, buying food for me and my children. Musa rarely appeared nowadays with any support. I figured that he was busy trying to support the other children he had fathered in Burlington, and I stuck to my word and did not go asking for money from him again.

Things went on like this for a time, family members came and went, until it was only my eldest brother and I left at home. But soon enough he decided to get married and leave also; although this is not the way it should be done. It is not right for the eldest son to leave the family home: he should have brought his wife home, where he would carry on the family line. He insisted on leaving to build his own home. The whole family argued about it, but my brother refused to listen or change his mind. I asked him to stay, but he refused to look me in the eyes as I did. Later he packed up his things and left.

Now I was alone in the house. I did not understand why everyone kept leaving me and I could not help but wonder whether there was something wrong with me, but I never came to any conclusions. I hated being in that house all alone, and so I decided that since everybody else was so good at leaving, then I would also.

I packed my bags and left the house, first taking my youngest son to stay with my sister. My eldest was already in Durban, at school. My sister was not happy and at first refused to let me go.

'You must stay,' she demanded. 'The father of your children might still come for you!'

'That is certainly not going to happen,' I replied after my laughter had subsided. 'Besides everyone else has left, why shouldn't I?'

I wondered how she could still think it might come true after so many years. At least in my head I had come to my senses long ago. In the end my sister knew that there was nothing she could do to stop me and so giving Iyanda a huge hug and waving goodbye, I set off back to Durban for the last time.

It was easy to find a job in Durban and I started working straight away for an Indian family, looking after the house and their children. It was a live-in job, and I had a small room in their home. I was happy to be back, although I knew that it meant I was in close proximity to Musa again. I chose to avoid him as much as possible, knowing that it was not good for me to be near him.

Unfortunately it would not be long till I need not avoid him at all, and not seeing him would no longer be a choice. Musa was ill. It was my son who informed me. He had seen him in Burlington, looking thin and far from healthy.

'I called out to him, Ma,' he said, 'but he did not hear me, even though I called after him several times.'

I saw the distress in my son's eyes as he spoke and so I decided it was time I paid Musa a visit. It had been a long time since I had seen him, and I was not prepared for his altered appearance. I tried not to let him see how shocked I was or that I was affected by what I saw, and acted as normally as possible. If he noticed anything, he did not let on.

We talked for a long time. The last time we had talked in such a way we were still young and at school, with our whole lives ahead of us, before life and all its hurts had got in the way. He spoke of being together, me and our kids. They were the same words that he had been saying from the very beginning, but still he did nothing to prove his love. Yet for some reason this time it was

June Rose's Story

In death there is rarely noise, and in the room that day there was a heavy silence. I knelt on the ground where my dad lay, holding his hand in mine as he struggled to partake of his last breaths. I had been so sure that he was going to get better, but now looking at him, so frail and so weak, there was no denying that the end was near. I put the plate of food I had brought him aside, knowing there was no need for it now. I simply sat there holding his hand.

It was a scream that finally broke the silence, growing steadily louder in my ears, a scream full of anguish and pain. I did not know where it came from, but it penetrated the invisible wall that had shot up around me, protecting me briefly from the gravity of the situation. Then I realised that the scream was coming from my own mouth, and it brought me back to my senses. Yet soon there was no more scream in me, and silence returned to the room.

Taking in a deep breath, I sank back down beside my dad after having unexpectedly found myself on my feet. My body felt so heavy and having no energy to hold myself up, I allowed myself to slump over his body. I don't know how long I stayed that way. I knew nothing could be done for him now and I wanted to prolong the last few moments I had with him. I could not take it all in, no matter how long I lay there, my own body draped over his now lifeless one. Eventually I got up and went to get help, although I knew that it was already over.

As soon as they came to take his body away, I ran: straight out the door, past the funeral van in which they would take my dad, past all the people gathering around outside our home, curious as to what had happened.

I did not stop running for a long time. It was good to feel the breath in my lungs and to concentrate on the movement of my body rather than the torrent of emotions threatening to take me over. I was afraid that if I really stopped to feel them, I would never recover.

I wanted to run away from it all, as far away as I could, to a place where it was all just a bad dream. Sometimes now I wish I had kept running. I wonder where I might have ended up if I had; whether it would be a better place than where I am right now. But dwelling on what might have been does not change anything at all, and it was here to Burlington that I found myself running. I ran straight to my mum's house. I don't remember what I said as I barged in through the front door. In fact, I may not have said anything at all.

The day it had started was like any other. I had no way of knowing when I opened my eyes to the new morning that it would be the day my life changed forever. At that time I lived with my dad in Escombe, a suburb of Durban. Often I try and recall what I was doing that day, but I never can remember. Although I do remember that my dad was alone watching television in his room, waiting for his friend to arrive so that they could watch the football together. It was only when his friend arrived that I discovered that anything was wrong.

The door to my dad's room was closed, and the handle would not budge. Realising that it was locked from the inside, I shouted through the door.

'Dad, open up!' I called, but there was no response. I called again, a little louder and knocked sharply. I listened closely for any movement coming from inside the room. I thought that he might have fallen asleep and allowed time for him to stir as I continued to call and knock increasingly harder on the door. Still there was nothing. An uneasy feeling began to stir in the pit of my stomach and finally turning away from the door I went to get help.

I returned with my dad's friend. He had to knock down the door to get in; as he did, I saw my dad lying on the floor. I started to rush to his aid, but before I could, my dad's friend hurriedly pushed me back out of the door, telling me to go and get help. I looked at him momentarily and then back to where my dad lay on the ground, then a sense of urgency washed over me and I ran from the room.

Instinctively I went to my uncle's house nearby. I am not sure how he understood the words rushing out of my mouth, but somehow he made sense of what I said. We collected a Zulu doctor who came back with us, though by the time we got back my dad was sitting up. The doctor gave him some medicine, and I am not sure how much it helped but he seemed to get better for a time. Until it happened again.

This time we took him to the hospital, and discovered he had suffered from a stroke. When he came home, I became his sole carer. This time he was much worse. He was paralysed down one side and he ate very little. I had to coax him to eat anything at all. He lost a lot of weight, and as time went by he found it progressively more difficult to speak. In order to hear him at all, I had to get in close to his mouth, and only then could I hear his ragged whisper.

Towards the end, I barely left his side. I tried to occupy his mind by reading to him from my school books and showing him the pictures, but there was little more I was able do for him. I could only watch as he grew weaker, and as he did my fear grew stronger. I kept telling myself that he would be better soon. Forcing myself to believe it would not be long till everything would be back to normal, I think it made it all the harder when it was not.

I was sure that the medicine given to him by the hospital was working. I remember asking him if he was going to be ok and then convincing myself that of course he would be. I asked him what we would do when he was better. There were tears in his eyes as I spoke, but I chose to ignore what they meant. For while his spirit was strong, his body grew weaker every day, finally failing him, forcing him against his will to leave me behind.

The funeral took place not long after his death. When the day came I was sick to my stomach. I had not eaten a thing in days, nor did I care to. I did not want to believe that this was my reality, but whenever I closed my eyes I could see my dad, lying on his deathbed, a shadow of his former self. It was not a picture of him that I wanted to be left with and I tried to replace it with a happier one, but no matter how hard I tried, I could not pull one to mind. As the initial pain and shock of his death began to lessen, my good memories of him began to return and the bad ones began to fade into the background. Till finally one day I was able to see my dad's happy face again instead of the images of his suffering.

I know that no one is perfect, but I only have good recollections of my dad and as is often the case, they have merely got better over time. He was a good man and friendly too. He had a heart for the community and often put their needs before his; yet more than that, he was a very good father. He was not one to shout at us often and when he did, we knew we had pushed him too far. He listened to us when we spoke and whenever we needed anything he was there for us. As for me, I was so close to him. You know most people in my family would say that I am the quiet one, but if you were able to ask my dad if it were true or not, he would have answered you with a laugh. For when I was with dad I was anything but quiet. In fact I was really quite loud!

So when my dad died, my world turned upside down and absolutely everything changed. Not only had I lost my dad, the one person that I could truly count on and be myself with, but I also lost the security of my life with him. For when he died, I had no other choice but to move here to Burlington and live with my mum and grandmother, where my life is anything but secure.

A good word to describe Burlington is chaotic. You never know what is going to happen from one day to the next. I remember in the beginning, when I had moved to live with my mum permanently, it was the noise that got to me the most. Perhaps at the time it was because of all the thoughts and emotions raging inside of me, which were so loud that anything outside of them was overwhelming. But I could never get any peace or quiet to be alone with my thoughts. Although on occasion I welcomed the distraction.

It was worst at night. When all I wanted to do was shut out the world, shut out my life and welcome the short reprieve that a few hours of sleep could bring. But even sleep seemed intent on abandoning me, and lying in bed surrounded by my mum and my siblings, I was forced to listen to all the nocturnal sounds of the settlement. Music was the biggest culprit, existing as a thumping soundtrack for those spending their nights drinking beer or smoking *dagga* (marijuana). The voices rose higher and higher as the night progressed, competing with one another to be the loudest.

Nowadays I am used to it, although I don't think that I will ever get used to all the fighting.

In Burlington, the men fight.
In Burlington, the women fight.
In Burlington, even the children fight.

The men fight over the girls, the women fight over the men and the children - well they simply copy what they see. I don't know who is worse! Although from what I have seen you could say it is the women. They fight dirtier, stabbing each other in the back with both their tongues and their knives. Sometimes I cannot believe what I see. My neighbours, friends and family treating one another so badly, not caring about themselves, never mind each other! Often I wonder who we as young people are meant to look up to? Who are we meant to learn from?

Then there is my mum who is always right in the thick of it, living her own hectic life amongst the chaos that is Burlington, drinking and fighting against everything and everyone.

My mum drinks: she drinks a lot. I don't remember a time when she didn't. Nor do I remember a time when our relationship was anything but strained. Sometimes I search my mind for memories that are different, for happy times. And there are some. You see, when my mum is having a good day, when she is in a good mood, I enjoy her. When there is no drinking and things are going well with her boyfriend, she is a fun person. We can sit for hours, laughing and talking, the way I always imagine other mothers and daughters do. Those are the times I hold on to with all I have got, hoping they will surface again. For such times pass too quickly, and soon enough she picks up a bottle again or her bad mood returns and I become the object of her irrational and often violent frustration once more. I never say anything. There is no point and it only makes things worse.

I want to shout at her; to scream at her to stop. In my mind I do, so loudly I think that my head might burst, but I never actually say it out loud. I know that if I do, she will lash out all the harder. I hate it; and I hate the feeling that constantly sits in the pit of my stomach. An uneasy feeling, persistently there, reminding me of the situation at home; it is there when I am at school, on my way home from school, when I am with friends, even more when I am on my own. I never know what I am going to come face to face with when I step inside our front door.

Yet it is my brothers and my sisters that I worry about more. They have never known anything different. Sometimes I see the look of fear on their faces and I wish so badly that things were different for them. That there was something I could do to make it all stop!

It gets bad sometimes. I feel the darkness begin to surround me, and my very thoughts begin to frighten me. I imagine the future, I try and figure everything out, but I can't. I think that if my grandmother dies, then I should follow. For even now, while my grandmother is still alive and able to help look after the young ones, I feel trapped. My siblings look to me, their sixteen year old sister, when they should be looking to their mother. But since she is not providing them with all they need, as the eldest I am the next best thing. But it is hard, as much as I love them and want to be there for them.

Sometimes I feel as though
I am suffocating
under
the responsibility,
confined
to live this life
here
in Burlington

when my dreams and my heart cry out for so much more.

Those are the times when I feel so weak, when it is all I can do to open my eyes in the morning and get through the day. I search for God but He seems so far away, so far from Burlington. But still He never fails to whisper softly in my ear; encouraging me not to give up but to dig deeper into Him, for it is there where I have learnt to draw my strength.

I grew up knowing God. My dad taught me a lot about Him. But it has not always been easy to love Him. It has not always been easy to see Him; it has not always been easy to understand. There have been many times when I have questioned Him and wondered where He is in my life. You see, when my dad died, it was not the first time that we had experienced loss as a family. It started when in quick succession my two younger brothers were both taken from us. Just when we were beginning to recover from the death of one, it happened all over again. I could see that it tore my parents apart and knowing the intensity of pain that I felt within myself, I could only imagine theirs. Perhaps it is this that finally caused them to separate for good. As for my dad I saw how he ached for the loss of his only sons and I know that with them, something within him died also. He never was the same again, I do not know exactly what changed, but it did. Not everyone noticed, but I did.

I was so angry with God at this time for the pain that I felt in my own life and the pain that I saw in my family. People would tell me that God had decided to take my brothers from us and I would think, 'How stupid is God!' I was in so much pain and could not understand how God was even there. He did not seem to do anything or help us in any way. However, in the midst of his own pain, my dad worked through it with me. He explained to me that my brothers were with God and sometimes we cannot understand why things happen, but we can hold on to the truth that God is good and He loves us.